35/
/250

1ˢᵀ

DIXIE DEATH DIARY

The Burial of a Southern Artist

LOCKE WOOD

Broken Boys with Brackish Blood:
Ghosts of the 7 Cities

A Civil War of One: The Battle of Manhattan
Virginia's Bastard in Brooklyn Bars

The South Don't Bury Its Dead:
A Return to Ruin

It's the Dogs That Still Haunt Me:
The Burial

Broken Boys with Brackish Blood:

Ghosts of the 7 Cities

Beneath a Burning Sky:
Barefoot in Blood

3 years old. 3AM.
A child's first memory,
the first vision of their bare feet
on this red-clayed Southern earth,
soaked with the blood of ancestral actions.
Maybe some American good.
Maybe some Southern evil.
What does that make that little boy,
in your mind?

American blood
lost for freedom and revolution.
Southern blood
lost for the wrong side of history,
a mixed legacy never left behind,
rooted in this land and his veins.

Pulled from bed,
rushed outside into
a field of swirling fog,
in the moonlight.
An old Virginia farmhouse.

Tiny bare feet scraping against
sharp bits of gravel,
sliding between his toes
entering the wooden gate,
into the open field.
The boy cutting through
the blackened blades of shiny,
sharp, and dewed grass,
flickering against small knees,
as he tries to catch up to his mother.

"Look up. It'll be here soon."

The child stared into the dark expanse
of Gloucester's night sky,
stars sparkling with the dying light,
in unison with the boy's sleepy swaying,
awaiting the comet,
a gift of the gods,
promised to him.

His eyes blinked, rubbed with his teeny hands,
scanning over the darkness for form in the void.
There lay the pale horse,
sleeping on its earthen floor.
A horse, lying in the grass,
odd, curious, unnatural to the child.
Weren't horses supposed to sleep standing?

Then, the revelation of the gods arrived into the sky.
The once-in-a-century comet screamed
through history as bringers of destruction, pain,
darkness, death, and war.

His mother wanted him to learn
the lessons from the ancients,
what was coming for him,
to see it firsthand.

The pale horse rose from the cold ground,
walked slowly toward the child.
The methodical movement startled the boy.
Its long neck bent down
to meet his gray-blue eyes,
as the comet died
in the sky above them both.

She would try to kill him.

Soon.
You'll see.

She was coming for him,
and the mother
wanted him to see it for himself.

Chambered Silence

He let a stranger at a bar
read his drunken poems.
They said, "Your words feel like bullets,
to my head. A machine gun."
They never mentioned them again,
their expression bleeding out.

However, the lead wasn't real,
the suffering remained cold in his hands.
When no one talked, he heard the chambering,
of words, of bullets. He hated silence,
it made him remember it all.
And he thought he'd make them remember,
if he could.

He wanted to squeeze his triggers
and make them feel his pain. It ate him alive.

A compulsion to blow their brains out
with each word to tell his trauma.
But that desire was never outweighed
by the destiny of a single shot
into his own head, a family tradition.

So he took a shot.

A Southern man knew his way around a gun.
A drunk Southern man knew his way around a pen.

He wanted to give context to his relationship
with the American right to bear arms.

He wanted to recount the first time
a loaded gun was pointed right at his face.

Where he was from, raised on the southern coast of Virginia,
threats to one's life happened more than one would like.

The 7 Cities, they called it.
The 7 Levels of Hell, he called it.

Level 1: Suffolk
Level 2: Chesapeake
Level 3: Virginia Beach
Level 4: Hampton
Level 5: Norfolk
Level 6: Portsmouth
Level 7: Newport News

Midnight murder mornings in Newport News.
Downtown Bloods, Uptown Crips, Norfolk crack pushers,
Hampton coke dealers, his weed dealer T.P., Aqueduct Killers,
Dynasty Raiders, any violent representative,
of their shared geography.

Even moonlit moonshine,
backwoods bastard country boys
coming in from the Blue Ridge Mountains out west.

The good ol' boys in pickup trucks with Confederate flags,
weed, guns, and revenge for frat parties gone wrong,
for pride bruised, someone looking at someone else's girl,
another cardinal sin of the South.

That year in Newport News,
there were 1,966 violent crimes reported,

meaning every day, anyone walking out that door,
they could have been, one of the lucky five victims
that the streets of the 7 Cities changed forever.

And 1,966 were only the crimes reported to the cops.
He didn't know many, if any, residents
rushing to call the cops to the scene.
Not one blue or red light flickering
in the aftermath of violence, usually.

The sights and sounds of streets went dark
after the blood spilled out. Only the sound of footsteps,
running away on blacktop, fading into the sounds of the city.
Calling the cops was an unforgivable sin.
If they happened to show up, run or go blind.

His blind eyes would witness a violent act
or the threat of a violent act at least twice a week,
most weeks more than that.
That hyper-violence created a hyper-vigilance
in a developing brain only ones from
that type of environment could fully understand.

If one found themselves in that
suffocating space one day,
here were some rules to survive:

Open Space
Be aware of all spaces. All of them.
Structures, architectural layouts,
walls, positioning, exits, furniture,
people, movement of lights,
movement of shadows, barriers,
weapons in view, possible hidden weapons,
to use, or to use against you.

Keep a safe eyeline
from anyone you don't know.

Sit or stand facing the door,
wall to your back.

Watch all entrances
and who enters and exits.

Never ever let anyone close enough
to touch you, or get behind you.

If things escalate, or the mood changes,
strike first or know how to unexpectedly counter.

Hands
Watch everyone's hands,
but don't make it obvious.

Jackets with no gloves mean
nothing obstructing the fingers
when they need to pull a trigger
or grab a blade.

Careful if they reach behind their back,
feign a stretch behind them, or fake
a scratch on a waistline.
Knives can be grabbed from pockets and socks.

Eyes
Read the eyes.
Movements, twitches, shiftiness.
The rate of their eyelids blinking.

Fast means nervous
and could trigger unexpected fighting aggression.
Slow blinking, or no blinking,
means a predator with focus
is looking to strike at the first vulnerable moment.

Mouth

Beware the mouth, fake coughs hide
razor blades in cheeks and under tongues.

Never share an opinion
out of your mouth
on anything,
until you read the room.

Be the quietest in the crowd,
and let your enemies and friends
tell you who they are.

Watch what you say, how you say it.
Tone and inflection.
It's a language unto its own.

Body

Watch what you wear on your body.
Attention is not what you're looking for.
Bright colors, big font lettering on shirts,
colors that could represent gang
or crew affiliation, what sports team
is on your hat or jacket, get to know the flags.

Be mindful to how you move your body,
and position yourself to the world.
Watch how you walk, too much swagger
makes you a target and its probably
insecurity driven 99 percent of the time.
Check your inauthenticity and fake ego,
it will make you easy prey.

Know when you're tough and know when you're not,
Don't slink down to the ground either,
you don't want to be too easy of a target,
just enough posture to make you forgettable,
one of the crowd.

Only look down at your feet when you know,
what shoes to step on and which ones not to.

Nose
If you smell alcohol, drugs, fear, desperation,
jealousy, anger, chemicals, sex, shit, fire.
Don't put your nose where it doesn't belong,
unless you smell betrayal, in that case, act.

Gut
Anxiety and fear can guide you.
If something's off, Trust it always.
Unless it's a subconscious trauma response
that's lying to you because of
neurobiological connections,
Explore that, master it.
It could save your life.

Head
Keep yours about you.

Dick
Keep it in your pants, for at least a few weeks,
when someone's girl is fresh out of a relationship
before you decide to spend some time inside her.
Unless you want a gun
pointed at your fucking face.

At 17 years old, in the shadows,
of the 7th level of the 7 cities,
the man, as a boy, sat on a stained swivel chair
in the cold chamber of an abandoned auto garage
on the edge of downtown Bad Newz.

"Nothin' but Bad News happens in Bad Newz,"
or "Newport Nam," as they called it back then,
a city that carried the heavy weight of a humid war zone,
reminiscent of the Vietnam War decades earlier

Chuck's ex-girlfriend was on the boy's lap, straddled.

Chuck scraped the barrels of the shotgun past her cheek,
and the boy found himself staring down the metal
of a wood-grain Remington 12-gauge shotgun.

The duct tape-wrapped stock gripped tight by Chuck.

(No relation to Bubba Chuck.)

Chuck got his shotgun from his older brother, D-Rock,
before he was sent to prison, a family curse.
D-Rock's sentence was longer than
an Allen Iverson NBA stat sheet.
That's just how the Commonwealth
handed down justice back then.

The boy nudged the girl off his lap.
She stumbled to the corner, visibly shaken,
her nerves unraveling in real time.

The boy scanned the garage for any accomplices,
his eyes sweeping over the shadows and corners,
before locking onto his would-be reckoner.

Deep inside, he knew, it wasn't his day to die.

And even if it was, he'd made his peace with it long ago.
He'd never known a time, not up until that moment,
where he wasn't okay with the end. Life had ensured that.
That's what this life had done to him.

He looked at Chuck, steady as a stone wall,
and said, "Don't do me any favors, my man."

Deep breath. Action.

"I'm a gangsta son, you don't fuck with me white boy!"

his new enemy calls out.

Deep breath.

Blood rushes to the boy's dick,
His cock's getting harder.
Adrenaline. Sex. Fear.
Violence. Mortality.

He's been here before,
in the dirt pit as a kid,
buried alive.

The dirty mix of life and death,
a fucking will to live,
a will to die, to end up
getting fucked and fucked over.

His senses become in union with Chuck's.

His fixed pupils to Chuck's
quietly quaking eyes,
His smirking calm against Chuck's
grinding teeth, gnawing
for a final reckoning.
The ultimate get back.

Chuck flips the safety off,
The click down
echoes through
the empty auto garage,
the chamber of cold steel and silence
and bounces off the
pull down metal doors in the back
ricocheting back
into the boy's ear drum.
It carried the weight of God's judgement
in this peninsula purgatory.

In that shuttering silence, the click,
something else clicks,

If you take aim at the boy,
with ill intent,
make sure that it's true.
And make damn sure
you hit your mark.

Because if you don't hit him,
You're as hollow as the point
of that bullet.

And the girl you love?
After he's done with you,
she still gets fucked.
But don't fret.
Because his girl will
eventually get fucked too,
by someone else.
Bigger. Badder.

It will always happen,
in this life.

Which leads him with a warning
to your…

Heart
Don't ever lead with it,
unless you get off
at watching it break.

Christmas on the Killing Fields

The internet places things into context,

if you look for them, and put it all together.

The boy was four years old,
eight months after the comet-of-the-century
and the pale horse of premonition
warned him of his end.

Patchwork memories were buried deep
for years to be excavated
atop the Yorktown Battlefields,
where 18th and 19th century
ghost soldiers roam the killing fields at night,
chasing whitetail deer with bayonet rifles
and thousands of fireflies
to light their way
back into this world.

The day was just over 200 years since
America won its independence from Britain
on this land, and here was where he began,
to learn about his own.

On an overcast Christmas morning,
the temperature sat at 47 degrees Fahrenheit,
97 percent humidity.
The wind gusted in
from the west/southwest,
whooshing over his head
and out over the rippling York River.
where the ships are sunk.

Phantom gusts dove down over the shipwrecks
at 12 miles per hour.
and into his red, chubby cheeks,
as fast as a bat; baseball or the animal.

He stared blankly, confused,
his hands stuffed in his puffy

Carolina-blue jacket pockets,
standing outside the first story
of a small townhouse complex.

Colonial crumbles of red brick scattered
over the edges where it lined
the concrete walkways toward
the entrances of each home.

A pale white painted front door,
A familiar equine color,
swung wide open, and all
he remembered
was a darkness.

No carpet.
No couch.
No side tables or televisions.
Just the shadows.
Until the EMTs wheeled his Gran out, dead.

There was a man sitting in his truck,
smoking a cigarette watching it all.
The boy didn't recall the cigarette itself
as much as the smoke hitting the cold air,
through the cracked window.
The man had the radio loud enough to hear,
but respectfully low enough
that no one mentioned it.

It was a tune that would repeat in his head
as a kid, whenever he needed to self-soothe,
alone in his room,
or when stress pressed him into silence.

Dada ding, ding,
dada ding, ding, ding,
dada ding, ding,

dada ding, ding, ding, ding, ding.

When he gained access to the internet, as a teenager,
he searched for the most popular songs of that year:
He found the song in a downloaded mp3.
The Final Countdown by Europe.

If you do the same,
you might realize,
the internet places things into context.
If you put it all together.

The Reaper Smokes, Jesus Drinks

A man asked him today
if he believed in the devil.

He said,
"We all believe certain things
at different times in life."

When he was a kid,
he used to think a man,
inside of a truck,
smoking a cigarette,
was the Grim Reaper,
here to claim a life.

The man said
he thought he might be related to Jesus.

He asked why.

The man replied,
"When I grow my hair out,
I look like him."

He said,
"That's good enough for me."

Jesus asked
if he was sober.

He was.
But he wished he weren't.

R.I.P. Current: A Bottlenose Baptism

At twenty-one, he'd get drunk
and swim in the Atlantic Ocean,
the north side of Virginia Beach.

There were a couple of go-to local beaches
where summer tourists wouldn't tread.
No loud music, no kids,
no lifeguards, no one to save you
American Southern freedom to live or die.

One summer day, while his girlfriend suntanned
on her towel, he drained his water bottle
of rum and Coke and wandered into the ocean.

It felt like a scene from a movie,
a Christ-like figure walking into the water,
arms stretched wide, baptized for his sins,
wounds healed.

The waves crashed over him,
seaweed and fish brushed against his legs,
as he waded deeper, and deeper still,
until he was fully submerged.

Head underwater.
Silence.

He cherished that.

He surrendered to the quiet,
letting the waves take his body
wherever they wanted.
That day, beneath the surface,
he heard something break through
the hum of the ocean.

A clicking, a chattering,
a whistling in the distance.

He lifted his head above the water,
dorsal fins cutting slow circles
through the top of the ocean.

Back down he went,
swimming toward the sounds,
surfacing for air when needed,
but going back underwater quickly,
afraid to lose the pod.

He just wanted to be close.
He didn't think much about it.
He just acted, a primal,
mammalian connection.

He even tried to mimic them,
clicks and gargled whistles,
a language learned
from childhood movies.

It was playful, childlike wonder
taking over, a magnetic pull,
to connect, to follow, to play.

But the closer he swam,
the farther they moved away.

The calls stayed distant,
always just out of reach.

But drunk and determined,
he kept swimming,
a youthful belief,
he could close the distance.

He turned towards the beach,
looking back to the shore,
over the rising waves
to gauge his position.
He couldn't see his girlfriend,
the coast was too far away,
he'd drifted far down the beach.

A sobering moment of mortality.
His body tensed.
His heart raced.
He turned around, kicking hard,
nervous but not panicked.
Focused.
He needed to get back to the beach.

But the rip current had other plans.
Fingers of the ocean gripped tight,
wrapped around his ankles,
dragging him deeper
into the Atlantic's depths.

He swam sideways,
diagonal, parallel to the coast,
anything to escape death's clutch.

Stroke by stroke, his energy began to drain.
His Marlboro Light menthol lungs burned,
salt water jamming into the back of his throat,
gasping for air.

He kept fighting,
kicking the current away,
trying to break free.

But then, the final thought finally came:
This was it.
His will wasn't broken,
but his body was giving up.
The ocean his ancestors crossed,
Is now taking their fatal fare back.

With the last strokes of his arms,
gravity splashing down,
fingers spread,
pulling at the water
like clawing out of that dirt pit,
one more stroke.

And then it happened.

He earned respect from Poseidon
and earned his life back.
The current released him.
The waves turned indifferent,
cradle-rocking him,
carrying his exhausted body
back to the beach.

Scraping his skin
with jagged rocks and broken shells
at the shoreline.

He lay there, muscles twitching,
fire burning through his arms and legs,
gasping for breath.

The sky above him was clear and blue.

It felt six feet away,
but for a moment,
it stopped pressing down.

Seagulls swarmed above, crying out.
His girlfriend's radio echoed classic rock
down the beach.

When he finally staggered to his feet,
he oriented himself on the coast,
dragging his feet
through the burning hot sand.

He found her, lying on her stomach,
unbothered by the world.

The thump of him collapsing beside her
caught her attention.

Without looking at him, she asked,
"Will you rub oil on my back?"

"Sure," he replied,
as if nothing had happened.

Still caught in that surreal space
between life and death.

He doesn't know how he made it.
He hears about drownings on the news all the time,
but somehow, he's still here.

Sometimes, he wonders if he did die that day.
If everything after,
this life, this existence,
has been something else,
some other space and time.

Maybe that's why baptisms
thrust you underwater first.
So you can die to be reborn.

He wanted to believe so badly.
He wanted to be connected.
He wanted to belong.
He guesses he was always willing to die for it.

A Honeysucker

In the 3rd grade,
a group of kids told him there was a witch
that lived in the woods
behind his elementary school.

He asked one of the kids
to show him the witch.
He wanted to be a part of the group.
Desperately.

At recess, on the edge
of the field where the kids were released,
unsupervised or minimally supervised,
the kid took him to the forest line,
to where the honeysuckle grew.

They picked some and sucked them.
A mix of honey and flower petals,
earthy undertones of the dirt
from the grime on his fingers.

There was a slightly overgrown path
to the left of the honeysuckles.
He asked the kid if the witch lived
down that path.
The kid told him to go find out.

The path felt like tides in an ocean,
pulling him toward the unknown connection
he had never felt but always needed.

So he did. He found out.

He pulled down the overgrowth from the entrance,
a triumphal arch of vines.
He puffed out his chest and headed into the forest,
not thinking long enough to worry
about the consequences
of an 8-year-old wandering in the woods.
But he was determined to belong.

The kid followed him down the path
and pointed out,
in the clearing of the woods,
an old abandoned house.
Vines climbing the walls, boarded-up windows,
a crumbling red brick chimney.

He stretched his arm and pointed
his dirty finger toward the hole in the roof.
He saw the dark silhouette of a witch
fly out of the house through the hole,
mounted on her broom.
She was flying up and to the left.

To this day, he vividly remembers seeing her,
the silhouette against the sky.
No details but the black void of light
in the shape of a witch.

She moved fast. He really believed he saw her.
He had to see her, to belong.

He fell to the ground.

"The witch got me!
She's going to kill me!" he proclaimed.

He wanted to believe so badly.
He wanted to be connected.
He wanted to belong to the crowd.
He guessed he was always willing to die for it.

Crossing the Lines:
A Southern Tale of Revenge

It started with the brawl.
An open field,
the meeting point between two worlds,
poverty and privilege,
a city line apart.

Eighteen, nineteen, twenty-year-olds,
trembling with rage and disrespect.
One side felt slighted,
something valuable stolen from them.
The other side outraged
that these outsiders would cross their city line
for retribution.

Their hands clutched pipes, bats, chains,
whatever they could grab from their fathers' garages.

They met in the middle of the grass,
next to an elementary school.
Calling out for violence as
they played their instruments of pain,
an orchestra of teenage savagery.

The first strike landed,
and the rest followed like a Virginia hurricane.
Whirling Chaos. Violence.

The inevitability of outcomes.
And then, in the distance,
the southern sirens began to sing.

By the time the cops arrived
and their guns pulled on innocents,
the field was empty,
blood-soaked grass and abandoned weapons.
The echoes of the fight were swallowed
by the silence of escape,
no one would tell, except the ones that
were left behind, demanding medical attention.

But the irony of it all?
The only one taken to the hospital
was the kid who came looking for revenge,
dragging his friends from the county to the city,
only to get his ass kicked.

The papers would write about it the next morning:
"Police Respond to Mob Armed with Bats,
Chains, and Crowbars. No Arrests Made."

But they were long gone by then.

Later that night,
blue and red lights flickered,
illuminating the '96 Chevrolet Suburban.
gunmetal gray.

Tinted windows rolled down slowly,
hands slipping out into the humid
summer night air.

His first, then Bobby's, then Mack's.
At 2 a.m. in this city,
in a tinted-out SUV with subwoofers
thumping in the back,

they were already guilty,
just by being present,
even if it was just for
"failing to come to a complete stop
at the stop sign."

Two officers shone their flashlights
through the tint of the back window,
creating three shadows.
They slapped the back of the Chevy
with their hands,
leaving fingerprints behind.

Probable cause didn't matter,
at this hour,
in this place.

They were cuffed for detainment,
but there were no weapons in the vehicle to find,
no drugs in their pockets,
just the weight of knowing
how quickly it could have gone another way.

Bobby didn't get so lucky.
Eventually, he put a gun to his own head.
Mack? He died far from here,
on some foreign island even further south,
mysteriously gone.
Just a post on social media announcing it.

And the third man?
He dies a little more every day.

The only friends worth talking about.

The Last Day the Sky Was Far Away

A few months after his Gran died
on the Yorktown Battlefields,
he was the next to be laid upon death's door,
on the Smithfield dirt,
bleeding out like a butchered Smithfield pig,
his lifeblood soaking the light brown dust.

The world turned dark,
the ground beneath him saturated with DNA
from the left side of his tiny, five-year-old head.
Exposed southern roots.

His older sister,
in the icy, detached way
that only she could manage,
always told him it was his fault.
He was an idiot for getting
behind the back of a horse.
He should've known better.

The same pale horse in the field,
the one that locked eyes with him
during the comet,
fulfilled her prophecy.

Unsupervised, he wandered behind her,
and she delivered her promise.
Her kick was her scythe,
slicing him for the world to feast.

The force hurled him through the air,
some untold number of feet,
into the trunk of an old Virginia live oak.

Unconscious, bleeding out,
barely breathing.

His mother ran for help,
while his sister stood by,
watching his soul cling to his body.

Baby face turning blue,
he lay in the back of the beat-up,
blue Chevy van,
speeding towards the hospital
across the James River.

His father wasn't there.
His superhero dad
was at the theater,
watching the He-Man movie,
Masters of the Universe.

"Alone," so he told his wife.

A few months after that day,
the day his son barely escaped death,
He-Man walked through the side door
of their country home.

He was told to get outside.

His sister rushed him out,
through the wooden door
with black-arrowed hinges,
leading to the small garage.

Three steps down,
three steps to the outside,
then a tight right to the front,
giving him an unobstructed view
through the bay window.

Inside, his father sat
at the head of the table,

facing his mother.

It was his resignation,
quiet and cold,
from the position of head of the household.
Seated across from his wife,
he declared his intent to leave,
to begin a life with her,
his wife's coworker,
her softball teammate,
his 15-years-younger new bride.

There was no anger, no emotion.
The glare on the bay window reflected
the stone faces of two people
witnessing the final fracture.

When he left,
he slammed the door so hard,
red brick crumbled to the ground.

That day, he took everything.
And the boy never got back
what his father ran away with,
no goodbye, no sorry,
no see-you-later,
not even a fuck-you or a truth.

Though his father always claimed
to be a Josey Wales kind of man,
he proved otherwise.
He took everything for himself
and left his choices behind.

The boy stood in the yard,
hearing the gravel crunch
under the boots of the man
he once called Dad.

It was a sound he'd never forget.

The man was a rattler.
A northern rattlesnake.

Looking up at the sky,
he saw the clouds shift and gather,
and the weight of them pressed down on him.

That was the last day he could remember
when the sky felt far away.

Ever since,
when he looked up at the Virginia sky,
it felt close.
Too close.
Suffocating.

The anxiety pressed down,
cutting into his skull.

The scar is still there.
You can see it
when he shaves his head.

Years later,
he found an old photo at his mother's house.

In the picture was the pale horse,
running through the same field
where he'd seen the comet burn bright
before fading out.

Just like his father did.

And his name that sat on her was Dad.
And Hell followed with him.

A Soul Patch & An Eagle Talon

The first time the boy got arrested,
He was 16 and got caught stealing.
not for the larceny or,
maybe even grand larceny, depending
on the statute of limitations on that one.
He was used to walking away with it,
and not getting caught.
Got lazy, too cocky.

But for some petty bullshit shoplifting prank,
with his friend,
he got cuffed up, in the stock room,
and got perp-walked out of the store,
in front of some classmates and their parents.
He tried to escape in the backseat,
planning on running
and using a grinder to get out of the cuffs,
but he couldn't quite get them
around the front of his body,
even though he could pop
his shoulder out a little bit.

His friends ditched him once the cops came,
he got it.
He would have done the same if he had to.
No use everyone getting taken down.

He went to court a few weeks later and
got sentenced to community service.
A bunch of hours washing cop cars
at the battlefields
with fellow juvenile delinquents.
The dude assigned to watch them
was in his late 20's, had a soul patch,
and a penchant for young women.
He said he put his two weeks notice in

and he doesn't give a fuck what they did.
Just don't make it obvious.

He let them smoke cigarettes,
and one morning,
Soul Patch brought the girl
to the gas station down the road
in his Eagle Talon to get some beer
'Cause she asked real nicely.
After smoking a cigarette
and sipping on a beer,
The graveyard 100 yards away,
3 generations of his blood
watched over him as he
took a long piss on the bumper
of the patrol car assigned
to the cop that arrested him.

Soul Patch gave him a thumbs up.

Mint Condition

His sister laughed
the loudest he'd ever heard.

When he was a toddler,
she said his breath smelled bad.

She gave him mouth spray.
He used it.

It was roach killer.

Hell's Little Ring Bearer

Later that year, after his father left,
they, not his father, stuffed him into a suit

and pushed him down the aisle
of a Catholic church in Norfolk.
As if this wasn't completely fucked up.

He stood in the hallowed halls
of Roman Catholicism's institution,
the same institution that annulled
his parents' union, the one
that brought him into the world.

By the Church's decree,
he shouldn't have even existed.
An unholy spawn of a marriage
that "never really happened."

And yet, the devil child himself
was assigned the job of walking down the aisle,
presenting a ring to his father
on a scratchy, cross-stitched Irish Celtic pillow.

A ring for a marriage that shouldn't exist,
delivered by a devil boy
who wasn't supposed to exist.

He had no faith in the performance.
They had no faith in his, either.
So someone made sure to sew the gold ring
onto the pillow, just in case he dropped it
and ruined everything.

He didn't remember much of the ceremony.
Mostly, he kept his eyes on the ground,
on the marble floors,
shifting his weight in those slick black shoes.
Slipping, seething,
the anger simmering just below the surface.

The bitch in white didn't help.

She was different from his mother,
different even from his emotionless sister.
This woman was something else entirely.

Her vacant eyes,
her words blistering and cruel,
spitting out like venom
from her herpes-scarred lips.

From the moment they met,
she had something to prove.
It wasn't just about thieving his father;
it wasn't just about replacing his family.
No, she wanted something more.
She wanted to break him.

And he could see it.
Even at that age, he could see it.
She knew he was the only one
who wasn't going along with the act.

When his father kissed the troll,
and yes, with tongue,
he wanted to bolt.
Run past the rice,
reach the car,
and escape into the backseat
of the rental.

He glanced at his ten-year-old sister,
sitting beside him, clutching a piece of paper.

"What's that?" he asked.

"Directions to their hotel," she replied.

He didn't hesitate.

Snatching the paper out of her hands,
he ripped it to shreds.

A million illegible pieces,
a million visible *fuck yous.*

He tossed the fragments out of the car window,
letting them scatter into the wind,
lost among the white of the rice.

For the first time, he felt the thrill
of his own form of justice.
His first taste of vigilantism.

Of course, his act only reconfirmed
his status as the devil child
to the demonic bride.

And the Roman Catholic Church,
cosigned it all.

In the name of the Father,
the Son,
and the Holy Spirit-Amen.

No reception for the devil boy.
No purgatory, either.

Just the hell they brought him into.

The Stone King

He didn't remember Kindergarten,
but his first memory of school was from First Grade.
Maybe it was because of the kick to the head,
he never saw a neurologist.

His teacher, with her leathered face and sharp glare,
would sneer at his cluttered desk.
Her clogs thumped the floor, circling him,
like a sumo wrestler slamming their foot,
ready to crush their opponent under the lights.

"Gross. Slovenly. Sloppy penmanship,"
she would say over and over,
until his head would drop,
heavy under the heat of her spotlight.
It burned his skin, reddened his face.
"You must have a kept workspace here."

He felt the judgments of his peers,
layers of Elmer's glue sticking to him,
slowly drying, cracking, peeling,
but never hardening enough to shield him
from the daily shame.
It was a ritual now,
his world watching on
as his humiliation unfolded.

One afternoon, as he sat quietly,
awaiting another trial of shame,
she announced a class-wide contest for lunchtime.
But he remained in the fog of disassociation.
This contest didn't apply to him.
Winning wasn't something
he'd come to understand yet.

The teacher then began telling a fairy tale:
the story of Stone Soup.

A group of starving travelers,
begging for food,
arrived at a town of well-fed, selfish folk.
Turned away for their
"disgusting" desperation,

they retreated to the woods,
gathering sticks for a fire,
stones for the pot,
and river water for their cauldron.

With a boiling concoction of nothing,
they proclaimed it to be
the most delicious, filling soup
in all the land.
"This single bowl," they cried,
"could nourish a family for days!"

Curious and prideful,
the townsfolk approached.
"What's in it?
Does it taste good?
What's missing?"

The beggars responded:
"This soup is hearty,
but it's missing just one thing
to make it perfect."

One by one,
the townspeople ran home,
returning with meats, spices, vegetables.
Each ingredient was added to the pot,
their bounty claimed by deception
and manipulation.

The beggars feasted for days.

When the teacher finished the tale,
she announced the lunchtime contest:
Stone Soup would be served.

She went desk to desk,
pouring boiling-hot, dark-brown liquid

into wobbly paper bowls.

A single stone rested
at the bottom of one lucky student's soup.
Whoever found it would be crowned
"The Stone King."

When they were finally allowed to eat,
he grabbed his plastic spoon
and dug in immediately.
Boiling droplets splashed his face.

And then he felt it.
The weight of the stone
at the bottom of his bowl.

Lifting it from the steaming pit of brown,
he revealed a sharp, jagged rock,
a relic that had traveled millions of years
to bring him this moment.

In that instant,
all judgments, abandonments,
self-loathing, blunt force traumas,
everything,
washed away in stone soup.

For the first time,
the gods shined upon him.
The stone, his small salvation.
That moment became
one of the only times in his life
he felt pure joy.
It set the baseline for his understanding
of happiness.

His hand rose slowly,
afraid to be seen by the class.

The teacher walked over,
announced him as the winner,
then told him to prepare
for a handwriting test at the chalkboard.

He was to be the first to stand
In front of the class,
she kicked his desk,
rattling him back to reality.

The Quiet Ones

After the third grade, after his father left,
his mom couldn't afford to keep the country home
with its acre of land, even working two jobs.
It was too expensive and too much to maintain.
So, they moved back to Hampton Roads,
to a smaller house in a neighborhood,
next to a trailer park.

He never went to the trailer park, up until this point,
no reason to, he'd just watch the kids get off the bus there,
seeing how they got stigmatized at school for their parent's lot,
in the park and in their life.
But that was the extent of it.

Once he returned from his year long sentence
at his father's house,
he got himself a girlfriend who lived in the park.
So, he decided to step in,
hang out with her in front of her single-wide
after school a few days a week.
Her mom would come out sporadically,
say some mean shit about his girlfriend's father,
And go back inside.

Sometimes she'd approach the boy with a

cigarette hanging out of her mouth and
proclaim to the court, pointing at him,
"I don't trust the quiet ones.
They're the dangerous ones."

One day after school,
The mom invited him inside the trailer
with her daughter.
Immediately upon entering
she told him to sit the fuck down,
on the stained couch, pushed against
the thin wall separating the living space
from the girl's bedroom.
She told him to mind her NASCAR pillow covers.
Mark Martin? Maybe Rusty Wallace?
Definitely not Jeff Gordon-
she thought he was gay.

She walked into the messy kitchen,
grabbed a green plastic bong
and a hardcover photo album.

She told her daughter to get to her room.
She needed to talk to him alone.
The girl got up and left obediently.
Her mother threw the picture book on his lap.
"Watch your dick."
Laughing before hitting the bong, she demanded,
"Open it."

So, he opened it.

"Do you see those guys?"
He nodded. It was a collection of her
at motorcycle rallies with her biker club.

"Do you see their patches?"
He nodded again, flipping through the 4x6 photos-

her topless on the back of
some big motherfucker's Harley caught his eye.

"Do you know what that means?"

He said no.

"It means they'll fucking kill you
if you hurt my daughter.
They don't trust the quiet ones either.
You're quiet. I don't trust you."

She took another hit of the bong,
coughed up Virginia Slims and dirt weed.
Her body shook until her rose-tattooed tit
popped out of her deep-necked
Harley Davidson tank top,
stretching and hanging towards her belly.

She looked down, grabbed it,
shook it at him, like a wiggling
Sunday morning flapjack,
smiling.

She put her finger to her lips.

"Shhh."

Maybe she'd have to trust the quiet ones after all.

A Sign of Southern Hospitality

The first time he saw a gun out in the wild,
he was 15 going to meet T.P. in Hampton to get some weed.
He met him around the corner from the Coliseum Mall,
T.P. hopped in and said, "Hey, you like mix tapes?"

Now, he was already on edge,
'cause he had to be careful around T.P.,
and if he brought anyone around T.P.,
he'd get real particular about his name.
He knew T.P. meant Thug Prince,
and had a thing about people
getting his name confused with Toilet Paper.
T.P. threw him the bag of weed,
and he said, "Yeah, I like mix tapes."

T.P. pushed in a CD into the deck
and it was the first time he heard
Hard Knock Life by Jay-Z.
The album wasn't out yet,
He didn't know how T.P. got it, but T.P. had it.
He paid the man after the song,
T.P. said, "Keep the CD,"
and told him to hit him up again.

He hadn't had his license yet,
but he was close enough to 16 in his mind.
Still, he figured he better head home to get high.
He never really loved it out in the world anyway ,
and by 15 years old, he was okay with disconnecting,
in his room, away from all of this..

He headed out, turned out of the backstreet, towards home,
approached a stop sign at a four-way intersection.
The car ahead of him honked the horn
at some dude taking a half-a-second longer
than he supposed he should've.
And no sooner than a half-a-second later,
the guy was out of his car with a handgun,
pointing at the driver's face through his window,
loudly explaining to him,
the meaning of southern hospitality.

He was disassociated from it all.

It felt like he knew it wasn't his battle to be in.
The guy kicked the side door and got back in his car.

He went home, got high out of a Diet Coke can,
and watched a jumpy bootleg ECW VHS.

He never honks at anyone if they are taking too long.

Strictly Dickly

Her name was Elsy.
He met her for the first time
in The Oaks trailer park,
one summer day in Virginia.

She told him about the small farm
and the field behind her momma's trailer,
where her uncle goes to pick
the psychedelic mushrooms
from the cow shit patties.
He comes back stinking her trailer
up to high hell and she has to wash his
boots off with the water hose.

She asked him to drive her
around town to smoke some cigarettes.
She had a freedom about her he never experienced before.
She laughed and played with the radio
in her Limited tank top and frayed jean shorts,
suntanned ⅛th Native.
Wind whipping her hair with
Marlboro Red smoke and Love Spell perfume,
calling out between puffs how
Faith Hill and Shania Twain are beautiful but
not in that way cause she's "strictly dickly."

She asks him to drive her

to her friend's house in Fox Hill
It will be fun to jump
on the trampoline in her backyard.
They did. He watched,
she made out with her girlfriend,
So much for "strictly dickly."

He watched.
When she was done, they left.
She knew a place to go.
Fisherman shack with a dock,
by the water, near a marsh,
where her Uncle fished
and where no one
would be there at night.

She said she wanted to sit
in the backseat of his car
And listen to more music.
He obliged.
She pulled down his shorts,
and took his virginity before God,
and the cattails.

He shook like a leaf
He didn't finish.
She was cool about it.
She was always kind to him,
never took it seriously.

In retrospect, she never wanted
to be his girlfriend.
She just wanted to be nice.

She ended up a stripper
in the next town over.
Someone told him
she went by 'Diamond' now.
He could see why.

Skirts, Lies, and Videotapes

First girl he loved
Told him her ex-boyfriend
she met in a local AOL chat room,
was in his twenties,
jailed in military barracks,
dishonorably discharged
and a real fuck.

He would pick her up
when her parents fell asleep,
take her to a motel out of town,
to make videos of them together.

She begged him
in a handwritten note
with pink and purple inked hearts
to give her money to pay the ex off,
to get the videos back.
He convinced his mom
for a little bit of child support,
sold his bike, some CDs, and,
gave her every cent he had.

She broke up with him after
he dropped her and her friends off
at laser tag in Virginia Beach,
for a new guy to take her home.

Her older sister finally told him
she spent the money
on clothes at the mall.
First girl he loved.
He's been trying to
save them all ever since.

MTV into the Real World

When he was 15,
he got back home from re-upping
some weed, rolled a joint
and was playing
MTV in the background.

A documentary played behind
 the clouds of smoke
This one happened
to be one on abuse,
of the sexual variety.

When the smoke cleared,
the smoke cleared.
The dissociation dam broke and
the walls came crumbling down.
The hurricane of memories drowned him
inside of a body that he couldn't get out of.
Ever again.

All the senses remembered
and came alive
to kill him, to bury him
in the pit of red southern dirt,
Alive, to never tell the story,
and to destroy every hope that
he may have had,

at a normal life,
or relationship.

Death was the only thing left for the boy.
He no longer belonged here.
No longer wanted to be on this earth,
in this earth, swallowed alive by
the suffocation of evil men.

He wrote a letter goodbye
and called his mom for one last goodbye.
She rushed home and took him to the hospital.
They admitted him for psychiatric hospitalization.

They wheeled him into the observation room.
All white just like the movies.
Padded walls just like the movies.
Strapped him down just like in the movies.
They left him all night, alone, just like the movies.

The next day the nurse came in,
and said 'Happy Birthday'
She asked if he still wanted out,
he lied and said no.
They let him sleep in a joint room,
strapped to the bed, next to another fucked up kid.

He met with the psychiatrist,
and they threw a cocktail
of sedatives and SSRIs at him.
They sent him to the couch
to let it kick in for 7 days.

No call from the family for his week in there.
No birthday party when he got out.
No one talked about it again after he got out.
No one asked how he was and how he survived.
It was easier for them to survive that way.

So he went back to surviving,
traded in weed for booze and toxic love.
Keep reading.

A Babyface Comeback

At seven years old, after being buried alive,
a story for another time,
he turned to escapism and dissociation,
the natural reaction of a baby brain
trying to make sense of the violence,
the good, the evil of the world around him.

In the isolation of a country house,
with its five channels or so,
the hum of the
television
became white noise,
a comfort against the silence.

Alone in a back room
at the end of the hallway,
he discovered professional wrestling
on TBS, the SuperStation.

He'd sit cross-legged,
the old typewriter balanced on his lap,
fingers flying over the keys during matches,
frantic when the action picked up,
deliberate when wrestlers locked into holds,
like headlocks or abdominal stretches.

His typing was a mirror of his emotions,
and he wasn't just typing;
he was observing, decoding,
learning to read blinking eyes and emotional states
as though his survival depended on it.

His favorite wrestler was The Great Muta.
Though Muta was a "bad guy,"
that didn't matter to him.
He related to the villain,
the painted face, the hidden identity,
the blinding green mist spat
into opponents' eyes to secure victory.

Muta didn't fight fair,
and he didn't care.
He wanted to win, no matter the cost.

It felt familiar, empowering even.
Watching Muta was like reclaiming power stolen from the boy,
imagining spitting back in the eyes of his abusers.

Keiji Muto gave him hope.
Ric Flair taught him confidence.
Flair, "Stylin' and Profilin'"
with his big gold championship belt,
was a beacon of swagger and control,
even if it was just a show.

He'd mimic Flair's "Woooo!" in private,
donning a cheap robe to strut like the champ.
Wrestling became his escape hatch.

He watched,
not for the drama of the fights,
but for the hope they symbolized.

The ultimate beatdown,
the inevitable underdog story.
Matches like Sting versus "The Russian Nightmare"
Nikita Koloff at Clash of the Champions XV,
a hero battered to the brink of defeat
but finding a way to escape and win,

against the most impossible odds.

Escape was possible.
He believed it.
He just had to figure out how.

One day, he grabbed a wrestling figure,
dropped it into a plastic cup,
filled it with tap water,
and stuck it in the freezer.

He checked on it constantly,
waiting for the water to solidify into ice.

When it was frozen solid,
he'd remove the cup
and begin the rescue mission.

Brute force, hammering, stabbing with forks, chiseling,
always careful not to chip the figure itself.
Melting it with hot water,
adding salt and pepper for no reason other than desperation.
He even tried using his own body heat,
holding the frozen figure in his hands
until they burned from the cold.

Each rescue was slow, methodical,
and an art form of its own.
The precision mattered.
The figure didn't deserve pain.

As soon as he freed the wrestler,
he'd drop him back underwater,
fill the cup again,
and place it back in the freezer.

Over, and over, and over again.

Each time,
he tried to get the figure out faster,
smoother, with less damage.

Each attempt was a rehearsal,
a symbolic training
for the next time he'd find himself submerged,
trapped in the pit.

He was reverse-engineering his escape.

Each frozen figure,
every cracked layer of ice,
was one step closer to freedom.

Until the next time.
Until he could figure it out,
how to get himself out of the pit.
But quicker.

Pantera's Sugar Cube: A Vision Quest

The Lizard King's Awakening

He's in the 10th grade, skipped the last period
and decided today was the day to be like
Jim Morrison and become the Lizard King.

Let's fucking do some LSD for the first time.

He signed onto AmericaOnline,
and booted up his AIM messenger.
He was on, a senior with long hair and
Pantera T-shirts.

He sent him a message simple:
Lucy in the Sky with Diamonds.

Pantera messaged back immediately,
THE FBI CAN READ THESE!
GAS STATION IN AN HOUR.

Two hours later, Pantera rounds the corner
And heads up the street to the gas station
Where the boy's been sitting out front smoking cigarettes.
They quickly exchange the cash from hand to hand,
Pantera gets payment, the boy gets a sugar cube wrapped in
aluminum foil.

He headed home,
Locked the bedroom door behind him
And put on *The Doors In Concert Live* Double Album
Into his small cracklin' boombox.
He was ready for his great awakening
Into another realm of understanding,
Himself and the universe around him.

He was ready for the death of the ego,
The message from the gods,
The balancing of the psychedelic psyche,
The ancient panther to deliver ancient wisdom.
He pressed play, unwrapped the sugar cube,
And let it dissolve slowly in his mouth
As instructed by his guide.

After what he thought was an hour of waiting
For it to kick in and thinking the cube was bunk,
"The End" was skipping, it was 10PM, and
He'd been watching QVC for 5 hours.
And the lady selling jewelry
Danced for him like a charmed serpent in
Her lotus flower earrings with amber centers,
And beaded and braided waist sash.
The shamaness of his shopping,
His Lizard Queen, brought to him by Pantera,
The ancient wise one, from the senior class.

The Ballad of BMX Bobby

Bobby was his best friend.
Bobby loved BMX bikes
and fighting skateboarders,
listening to Hatebreed
and Blood for Blood.
He got a bike chain tattooed on his arm
and would bring his best friend moonshine jars
that he he stole from his dad.
They'd get fucked up, go to hardcore shows,
and Bobby would drive them around town
looking for trouble, telling stories,
claiming victories and earning wings,
like red ones for fucking on her period.

He was told Bobby was a compulsive liar
and not a good dude but he didn't care.
He loved Bobby, Bobby was good to him.
He didn't care if Bobby lied to him,
Bobby popped his back pimples,
stood up for him in a crowd,
and didn't look at his dick
when the Hungarian girl
was giving them both handjobs.
He called it Hungarian Blind Snow Skiing.

Bobby was Bobby
and took that Bobby energy wherever he went.
Bobby would as soon dump copious amounts of salt
in milk jugs inside some random kid's fridge at house parties
as he would shave his friend's head
before a prom he wasn't going to.
Bobby was Bobby
and Bobby loved BMX.

He'd drive over the state lines
to North Carolina for Dave Mirra's

BMX ramp in his backyard
whenever the guy was out of town on tour
or at some competition, break his chairs,
and leave an apology note
while pissing in the bushes
and telling the story.

Wrecking shit, talking shit, stealing shit, being shit
He was proud of that. He embraced the piece of shit culture.
Bobby was a good friend, even when he wasn't.
The boy loved him for that.

1993 Tombstone:

Turkey Creek Jack Johnson: what the hell you doin' this for
anyway?

Doc Holliday: Wyatt Earp is my friend.

Turkey Creek Jack Johnson: Hell, I got lots of friends.

Doc Holliday: I don't.

Bobby blew his brains out
in the front yard of his house.
Dave Mirra suffered the same fate.

The boy thinks about him
anytime he watches Tombstone
or sees an intoxicated mischief maker.

Every time there's a drunken fistfight
A Bobby gets his wings.

Dapped by a Dragon

After high school,
he took some community college classes over in Hampton,
selling a little weed while delivering pizzas from Cha Cha's,
and spending weekends with his best friends in Newport News.

Bobby loved hardcore music,
so one weekend, they went to see half a set
of *Bad Luck 13 Riot Extravaganza*,
until the crowd started destroying the venue,
pulling down ceiling lights, and a brawl erupted
and police shut it down.

Mack loved rap music,
he'd play leaked mixtapes before public release.
He was from New York, with a connection to the DJing world.
Sometimes on weekends, they'd sell a few CDs
at Patrick Henry or Coliseum Mall,
happlly pocketing extra cash.

His boy's brother worked in a pharmacy,
one that didn't seem to count pill bottles.
OxyContin cash flowed freely.

One weekend, he was called to Washington, D.C.
to see a person about seeing a person.
Bobby and Mack dropped him off at the train station
after partying late the night before.

On the train, he fell asleep until
the conductor's voice woke him,
"Richmond, last stop to smoke until D.C."

Groggy, he took a swig of water, stood up,
and shuffled down the aisle,
making sure not to step on anyone's shoes,
a rule of the street, learned in unpredictable

movie theater settings growing up.

Looking down, he noticed a problem,
a hard-on. It happens when you're young
and you wake up.
He quickly covered himself with both hands,
pretending to fiddle with his flip phone,
shuffling down the line until he got outside.

On the platform, he tucked it in his waistband,
bumming a light from a lady and her friend.
The cigarette brought him back to the waking world.

As he smoked, looking around the train station,
he saw a silhouette in the distance,
swaggering down the train platform.
The figure came closer.
Five-and-a-half feet tall,
walking like he owned the world.

The boy squinted, wiped his eyes,
trying to place the face.
Did he know this guy from high school?
Did he buy weed from him?
Does he know Thug Prince?
Sell weed to him?

The haze of the night before made it hard to tell.
Closer now, they locked eyes.
He took another puff of his cigarette.
Behind him, one of the ladies whispered,
"Is that Sisqo?"

Sisqo?
The guy with *that* song about thongs?
The one on MTV, flying in private jets,
Partying on yachts, not hanging out at train stations?
This guy didn't even have the famous platinum hair.

The smoke evaporated,
and the realization hit as he got closer.
"That's motherfuckin' Sisqo."

As Sisqo approached, their eyes held their lock,
When he reached him, Sisqo stuck out his hand.
He dapped him up.

"Sisqo, what the fuck are you doing here?"

"Man, I live in Baltimore," Sisqo said,
"and it's easier to take the train than fly."

The ladies behind him chimed in,
"Sisqo, Sisqo! Can I get a hug?"

Sisqo glanced at the boy, then at the ladies.

"Nah, girl, I'm trying to keep a low profile."

He walked back into the distance,
hitting his swagger stride,
rocking his Sisqo-branded dragon sweater
and matching Sisqo-branded dragon backpack.

A Civil War of One:
The Battle of Manhattan
Virginia's Bastard in Brooklyn Bars

A Token for the Truth

He wears it on his wrist,
ten years after leaving the South
to chase his dreams of being seen.

A wooden beaded bracelet,
given to him by a holy woman
on the streets of midtown Manhattan,
a robe, a warm touch on his arm.

In return,
she led him to the ATM,
a quiet, sharp reminder
of the nature of spirituality.
And so, he wears it,
a token of her words,
a warning etched into his mind.

That nothing in this life is free.

Not that woman's kindness,
not that bracelet,
and certainly not
his spiritual salvation.

LIFE Spread on the Floor

Cancel plans. The weekend.
He isolates himself from his world,
and sits in silence.
A white page, a black pen.
A white canvas, black paint.

He's tried to give the world a masterpiece.
Truly, he has.
But after all this time,

he guesses he never will.

He came to New York
Because the South
almost buried his dreams
alive in that pit with him.
And now when
pen hits page,
Nothing.
Paint hits canvas.
Nothing.
Bottle hits lips.
Frothing.
He's buzzed.
BZZZ. His phone vibrates.
A text:
"I wish you could feel how wet I am."
Sext after sext.
Naked picture after naked picture.

The greats, his artistic and literary heroes,
never had to deal with distractions like these.
Tortured artistic souls,
seeking to live in a time where passions
could thrive uninterrupted,
by the constant, default alert of an iPhone.
Just Nazis and Communists,
Not Nudes and Notifications.

Perhaps he was born in the wrong era.
Maybe 1940s Greenwich Village.
Maybe if he disavowed electronics,
went off the grid like the immortals.
Went celibate. Maybe.

His oversized touchscreen propositions him.
A blowjob from a stranger.
He submits to the pressures.

He remembers,
Jackson Pollock was 37 years old
when LIFE magazine gave him a spread.

He's got time, he tells himself.

But maybe this is his *LIFE magazine*,
spread out on the floor, drunk, alone.

As he lays on his side,
his arm going numb
under the weight of himself,
waiting for a knock on his door,
his head finally rests
in the place he always returns to.

Crawling back from the bathroom,
the tired, torn carpet beneath him.
His cheek pressed to the cold
wood panels exposed underneath.
This body aches for a break.

The studio above him sleeps.
The stranger below him sleeps.

They exchange glances,
sometimes the stranger even helps him out.
Once, the stranger let him back in
from the small patio space
where he'd locked himself out of.
But the stranger always retreats rapidly,
back downstairs.

He thinks they understand each other,
The silent deal they've made.
He respects him for that.

They hear one another's orgasms at night.

He makes more noise and
the stranger doesn't last very long.

He wonders if that's why
they don't talk.
Why they don't look each other in the eye.

If the stranger only knew
it's the beer and dissociation
that give him such a dramatic,
competitive advantage.

The stranger drinks beer too.
Lots of it.
He sees it in the recycling bin,
next to the stranger's empty cat litter boxes.

Fuck Me, Don't Save Me

A drunken streak
of northeastern snowflakes spit
and stream down the face
of a window, fading into the night,
a foreshadowing of this
late January day's end.

The Wednesday swerves
left into Thursday morning.
This is between them,
the bartender, the lone cook,
and the waitress he's been dating.
The bar locked the doors a while ago,
but Jersey won't take that hint,
because she's in her moment.

This is her life.

The waitress flips the stools over and
goes to sweep the floor
around where the two are at,
a little nudge to get the fuck out of there.
The Southern man gets it.
Jersey doesn't.

They turn off the music
playing over the bar's speakers,
and Jersey pulls out her phone,
starts playing her own playlist.
American classic rock from
the 70s and 80s,
explaining to the man
that she knows about music
because she used to be the help
for a certain rock n' roll superstar
from decades past.
She throws her jewel-cased phone
in his sightline to show him visual proof,
her and the rocker at his estate's Christmas party.

"Yep, that's him.
He doesn't look too happy."

She does a New Jersey fist pump in the air.
The man smiles politely.

The smooth-skinned Indian bartender
walks out of the kitchen with their food.
She widens her brown eyes at him,
as big as her tits that
she sent in a late-night nude picture exchange,
gently placing down the pub fries nacho dish
the cook threw together last minute for the man
as a personal favor.

They're friends, kind of.

She told him about her adoption
from India to a white family.
She subtly tried to fuck the man once,
but he didn't hold it against her,
and they only see each other at the bar.

At this point in his life,
I'm sure she wouldn't have been
too impressed by his drunken performance.
Too much in his head,
too much alcohol to even get there.

She gives the man free beer,
but he always tips her more
than what he'd pay for the beer anyway.
He chalks it up to the price
of 'knowing' the bartender.

The man tells Jersey he needs
to wash his hands before he eats,
heads to the bathroom,
and take a couple of inhales
from a mint vape rig he bought back in Providence
with his bipolar ex from Vermont,
She eventually left him
to become a lesbian.

He checks for any alerts
from other women
he's talking to on the dating apps
to validate his worth,
until they figure him out,
or until he backs out,
before the grand reveal.

He washes his hands
and stares in the dirty mirror to

adjust his hat covering his balding head.
He checks his slightly crooked teeth for anything
Stuck between the jagged overlaps,
And runs his fingers through his graying beard.
He tells himself under his breath,
he needs to get out of there and go home.
He works in a couple hours,
and needs to sober up.

He returns from the bathroom,
turns the corner,
back into the room where Jersey lined up
five shots of tequila in a row on the bar.

The man watches on as she takes
four of the shots back to back,
to the back of her throat.

He politely takes the last one on her insistence,
grab a few fries, and throws down
two twenty-dollar bills onto the bartop.

He smiles.
"It was truly nice meeting you.
I hope you have
an amazing night,
and please get home safe."

He leans in and gives her a quick hug,
exchanging unspoken messages with the bartender,
A wink at her, and heads for the door.

The bar is about to close and Jersey yells
in protest that people from New Jersey
party better than New Yorkers.

She screams out at me,
"Where the fuck are you from?!"

The man calls back,
"I'm from Virginia.
I don't have a dog in that hunt."

The door swings closed behind him,
Hearing her muffled voice
saying something,
but by the time he can make out
and process some of the garble,
He's a block down from the bar.

Then he feels the vibration of his phone go off.

It's a text from Jersey:
"I hate my life."

Fuck.

Now he knows he has to get this girl home safe.
Held hostage by the suicidal ideations.

He takes off his snow gloves, reaches in his
Over-washed black jeans, grabs a crushed box of cigarettes,
and lights a menthol American Spirit.

He readjusts his course back to the bar,

but Jersey has already headed him off at the pass,
zig-zagging down the street.

If only a straight line was a spiral.

The man sits her on the curb
And tells her it's all going to be okay,
that the cab will be on the way soon.

She screams about all the cocaine
she did this summer,

her ex-boyfriend being a dick,
and how much she wants him back,
crying into her hands.

He walks away a little ways from her
to call the taxi cab,
and the dispatcher asks where he's located.

He looks up at the street sign
for a pick-up spot:
a nightmare on Elm Street.

He quickly hangs up and tries to validate her feelings,
in all reality, lying to manage her, reel her in
until the cab arrives without her
walking in front of traffic or who the fuck knows what.

The yellow cab finally arrives and
The man opens the rear side door
as she stumble-dives into the backseat.

After about 4 prompts,
She finally tells the driver her address.
The man tries give the driver some cash
from outside the car
and attempts to close Jersey's door.

His duty is done.

She sticks her hand out
And blocks the door from closing.

"I'm not going anywhere
unless you come with me."

He looks at the cabbie defeated.
He looks at him like,
'Hey, handle this. This is your problem.'

Fuck.

He climbs in the front seat of the cab.
"Let's go."

She mumbles about the city,
more about Jersey and men,
until her stop mercifully arrives.

She leans over to the man's right ear
and whispers
"Fuck me, Don't save me."

She flings open the cab door,
gets halfway down her walkway,
and turns back.

Reaching into her purse,
she throws a wad of one-dollar bills at him
through the car window.

He says that it isn't necessary,
but she mumbles some more about
independence until she turns back around
Towards the front of her building.

He tells the driver to wait
until she gets inside.
She does and
He turns to the cabbie,
raises his eyebrows
And says, "please take me home."
"Have a good night?" he asks.

He chuckles,
"It's the glory days."

We get down the road,

and the man's phone lights up.

She texted him:
"Why didn't you come in and fuck me?"

He writes back:
"I have no idea."

He woke up the next day,
Drove 45 minutes in the snow,
hungover,
to help a heroin addict detox.

I think he believed in helping people,
even if you can't help yourself.

He said he was no hero,
just a piece of shit
that could have used someone
to pick him up before
an innocent stepped into it.

The Muse

He knows when he feels it,
It consumes him.
He's thrown into his obsession,
a magnetic, obsessive-compulsive
need to memorialize them,
for an eternity, through his art.

An ethereal connection,
shared in this moment,
so disparate, so rare,
they must be eternalized,
or be lost to time.
The most tragic thing

an artist can comprehend.

It's an equal exchange:
he etches them into the narrative
of existence, the human story,
this fleeting time on Earth.
And in return,
she shares her gift from the gods.

She's unbound by fear,
unafraid to explore the unknown,
to step where the light of humanity
intersects with the visceral tools of art,
and her shadows of her darkest self,
the ones she's only faced alone.

They're there together, trembling,
all parts of their selves,
integrated, vibrating,
a new frequency
not known possible
by each on their own.

A muse.
Swaying,
no footsteps,
her fingertips slightly lying
on his hips,
as the smoke danced,
danced off her lips.

Turning toward him,
in the center of the studio,
she dropped her holey cloak,
spelling out his future
with every breath.

She spoke slowly:

"If you cannot marry me,
then paint me and immortalize me.
And if you cannot paint me,
then write of me and immortalize me.
And if you cannot write of me,
then fuck me and turn me mortal,
in your mind.
And if you cannot fuck me,
then drink, to losing me."

She said, "No matter what,
we all have a choice."

And then, her gaze piercing,
into his eyes. She whispered,
a whisper meant to terrorize:

"I have given you four roads.
Now go
conquer
the whole
fucking
world."

A Ghost in Brooklyn

Brooklyn steel and East River wind,
he reeked of drunk sweats and jealousy,

The Gray Ghost appeared,
not in rattlin' chains
or singin' ol' hymns to the grave,
but in the way his fingers
clenched his glass,
how his jaw locked,
at the sight of her

flirting for fun,
for his fire,
for his hell of it.

It ain't just pride,
it's a possession wrapped
In misguided masculinity
it's covetous disguised as love.

it's all about leaving the bar
before you start swinging
and they start falling.

Cassette Single Symmetry

I saw a woman.
At the bar tonight.
She had
Flowing hair,
with blonde and brown highlights.

Isn't that what you want?
Can't believe that shit.
So beautiful.
Born into that.
That symmetrical face,
the symmetrical face.

She was talking about an IUD with her friend.
And kids. No ring.
So she fucks.
And you'd want to take her.
Shit, I'd want to take her.
But I played the tape out though.

Picture this:
The bullshit introduction.

The struggle,
The struggle of when her friend
went to the ladies room.

The convincing of her
that I'm different.
The art, the vinyl, the prose.
The tattoos,
the dreams of the doctorate.
The chaos
and yet
the security.

I've got her now.
I am not your man.
I am here to take you.
On my couch.
The grab of my back.
Leave that mark.

And YOU were the mark.
The pull you close to me.
The passion of
these blue eyes
bring you into me.

I don't care if you leave,
I really don't give a shit,
if you leave.

So I grab your hand,
into the bedroom.
And you come.
And you cum.
And you leave.

And
Then what?

You're gone.
And
I'm here.
And you were
just symmetry.

The Stone Throne Built on Smoke and Mirrors

Sometimes,
you have to put the crown on your own head,
like Napoleon in Notre Dame.

You throw on yesterday's clothes,
your scarlet and gold robe
scattered on the midnight floor of your chapel,
where countless nameless knees have hit.
Where desks once rattled, knees now bend,
dripping mouthfuls, slick with confession,
proving your worth.

After a full day of drinking and writing,
invading minds like a conquering Caesar,
your procession back into Rome
is a stumble down the road to the local bar.

Light a cigarette in the rain
and celebrate your reign,
for you are invincible.

You post up at the bar,
stare into the mirror
through half-empty liquor bottles
lined up for your choosing,
the spoils of war.

The bartender calls you honey,
and you catch it with a wink and smirk,

never catching her vinegar stare
when you look away.

You gaze at your own reflection,
and you know they're watching,
wanting to approach you,
to gain audience with the king,
but they give too many fucks,
don't know what to say,
their silence thick as glue.

And you?
You're the emperor
on your imperial throne.
You're Liberty, leading the people
The bottle and flag in your hand.

They're Delacroix and Ingres,
immortalizing your scene,
and you?
Sit for your portrait.
You're king, and never forget:
You're the motherfucking Stone King.

Clawing at Connection

She pushed him into the graffitied bathroom stall,
her lips still tasting like someone else's cigarette,

"You still believe in God?" she breathed,
He hadn't prayed in twenty years.

In their phones the world burned for the 1 percent,
inside, two stray dogs, fucking like the fucking
Animals they are, mounted in some back-alley,
next to the dumpster, clawing their way
into their backs, and back to something human.

The bathroom mirror was filthy,
in the reflection,
they couldn't find themselves,
finding themselves.

Riot for My Love

He learned as a child,
putting his action figures in the freezer,
that water hardens at 32 degrees.
In a New York winter,
with -12 winds,
a lit cigarette could make an icy woman
melt down in front of him.

At 3 a.m., his eyes cracked open.
It had been a long night of drinking.
Rubbing the grit out of his vision,
he rolled over to check his phone,
looking for anything to distract him.

A notification blinked:
"You've made a new match."
The algorithm, designed to draw him further away
from the things he actually needed to do,
reeled him in like it always did.

Earlier, he had stumbled home from the bar,
retreating into the frigid night.
The temperature plummeted,
17 degrees down to 6.
His worn black boots hit cold pavement,
while his face burned crimson,
beneath years of umber, raven, sand,
and now gray granite.

The bar was close to home,
near enough to his makeshift art studio.
It was a refuge where he could drink
a couple double IPAs,
meet someone new from an app,
have a few more rounds,
and then head home together for the night.
Or alone. Either way there was beauty in both.

Her words from earlier at the bar
clawed their way out from behind
the drunken haze of his bedroom:
"You can leave anytime you want,"
she had shot at him,
drowning in her own familiarity,
throwing her fake fur coat over his head.

He pulled the coat off his face.
"I can leave? I live here. How about you?"

Reaching for a pack of cigarettes
from his jeans crumpled on the floor,
he pulled one out of its crushed box
and lit it.
The filter stuck to his chapped lips.
Her eyes, dark as they come,
caught the flame
and swallowed it whole.
Her pupils expanded, overtaking her irises.
Her unemotional words became fire.

"Give me you!
All of you!
And I'll stay!" she belted.

Her gasoline smile ignited the fumes.
Wet lips curled into a smirk
as smoke filled the room.

He wanted to tell her
she didn't want this smoke,
but she'd brought the accelerant.

Her words: gasoline,
poured all over his bed.

She pointed her painted daggers at him
as she slowly began to move closer.
Her hands shot out,
wrapping around his throat,
her grip tightening with every cruel smile.

Then she threw a Molotov cocktail
straight into the front window of his act,
the one designed to burn his ego,
down to the ground.

She was rioting for his love,
leave him in shards
just to get at what was left.
Take what she believed she was owed.

She's been starved out by his systems,
she was going to get hers.

She climbed on top of him,
straddling him,
put him inside of her,
her grip tightening,
laugh after laugh.

Murderous Candy Eyes

She slowly glides his
knuckle upward,
toward his forehead,

forcing his index finger,
Extending into his temple.

Her manicured, press-on nails
dig into his wrist,
picking at his veins
like trembling
guitar strings
with her plastic picks.

She raises his thumb
with her own,
only to let
that hammer
drop.

To feel the sensation,
the peaceful end,
staring directly into
her
murderous
candy
eyes.

NO COMPARISON

And I have been
The Hurricane.
Lain Bare.
Right There.
Next to the Ocean, Atlantic…
The glass windows,
the shuttering,
your reflection shaking,
Shaking.
Until the Thunder,
Thunderous

Shattering…
With the Wind
Howlin'.
Wolves.

And I have been
The Earthquake.
Lain Bare.
Right There.
Standing Stories,
Left up in the Sky.
The glistening memories of us,
Flying Off My Wall.
As the earth trembles,
So Low…

And I have been
The Outside.
Lain Bare.
Right There.
In the Misty Coil,
Of Your Tornado.
Burnt clouds kissing at my feet,
Stealing Your Light,
posing as souvenirs.

So Come Close,
You.
And Come.
Close.
You.

I want you to hear all of this.
None of them,
None,

Darlin'
Come Close.

To the Rumble,
To: the RUMBLE…
Of You…
Lain Bare.
Right There.
Underneath Me.

The Alley's Way

Look at what
you have done.
Just glare upright,
as the rest look on,
as it all falls
into place.

No doubts,
no anxiety,
no adversity.
Life will pass you by,
with the swiftest, smoothest shift.

So.
Just smile for us.
Toss your hair.
Lay upon that face.
Lace up those boots.
Torn tights
that no one will notice,
but everyone will notice
and worship you for.

This pandemonium
of power
is with you now.

The dark alley of him.

Walking past
the barrels of fire,
into the alleyway
of him.

A red-draped smile.
A white-laden grin.
Stepping over
barely breathing bodies,
strewn through
city streets behind you.

The slip of your dress,
laid on the wet brick.
Your heels stuck,
sunk into
the freshly poured concrete.

Leaning down,
to immortalize your kiss.
Your lips for them
to tread over.
Taking pictures
to send to their closest.

Your cheek, shined
and dragged against
the permanent floor.
Your profile becomes
someone's profile.

Flashbulbs explode,
explode,
into your eye.
Trails of light
with every flash.

Press Send,

to me.

Folding for the Right Hand

He says he's too tired to screw.

This one doesn't lift her voice,
She doesn't throw an uppercut,
or cut his face,
She doesn't slam his car door
hard enough to rattle his frame.
She just says it real casual like,
like there's simplicity in decisions.

"Maybe I'll let the other guy keep me out
all night long next weekend. Cool?"
And that? For a southern man,
hits harder than any screaming match or 'Fuck You'.
Because she knows him, knows the card to play,
to get what she wants: him.

He shoots up, shakes off the
Captain Morgan cobwebs,
Grabs her to make it ever clear,
what's never gonna fucking happen.
She smiles. She got 'em.
And all of a sudden,
The boy ain't so tired anymore.

Confession

It's just me, you,
and three local
bar clientele.

Your eyes that I'm usually lost in,

but never showing you my true intent,
are now glassed over,
but we haven't had
one drink.

You're fucked up.
You finally admit it.
You admit
you had texted me,
last Friday to come out.
and I didn't respond.

You met up with a friend and
You needed to get drunk.
You tried to be good,
but you drank and
ended up in a hotel room,
that your friend booked.

She told you
she has never seen him
into someone
as much as he is
into you.

You did cocaine.
and Talked finance with Chet.
Your friends left
and you fucked.

The next day,
You rode to Burlington
and you slept the whole way,
While I made you art.
Your façade is impeccable.

He never contacted you again
and

I'll never contact you again.
I walk home.
Busy intersection,
I don't look both ways.
I look no ways.

I walk.
Car swerves next to me.
I feel the breeze but nothing else.
I could have died tonight,
in retrospect.
Paw prints in the snow.
I am home.
And I made you art.
with the tear-soaked muck.

The Lyin' Witch and Her Wardrobe: A Cocaine Ceremony

A Wiccan yoga instructor,
tie-dyed scarf, tie-dyed leggings,
and a diamond nose ring,
her husband in Dubai with the kids.

She disappeared into the bathroom,
the door slamming behind her, echoing
like an ancient drumbeat in the forest,
a call to announce,
the beginning of her ceremony.

A humming, melodic symphony
accompanied the chopping
of her ritualistic plant medicine.
A few lines of coke to commune
with the northern gods, peering down
from the heavens,
illuminating her in the flicker

of fluorescent light.

When she returned,
her face met his, biting his lower lip,
her mouth thick with cinnamon and chemicals,
her neck, lavender and weed.

Her hands tore his shirt over his head,
her movements intentional and fluid,
a ritual rehearsed.
She pulled his hand out to accept her offering.
Sliding her finger into her mouth,
she glided it against her tongue,
removing her wedding ring with her teeth.
She stared into his eyes,
placed the ring in his hand, and closed it.
Her movements rhythmic,
her breathing, a chant.

Her body circled behind him,
and he felt her presence heavy.
Her nipples carve into his back,
Her hot breath dragged down his neck,
each stroke of her sharp tongue,
tingling with residual coke.
Every lick made him wish
it were a ceremonial blade
to bleed him out,
not for her gods,
but for his.

Sacrifice him
for her moment.
Death is belonging.
Belonging is death.

Woman Reclined with Mask

Once there was a woman,
and she wore a mask.
As it was,
she would lean
and recline
at the head
of his bed.

One night,
just before
daybreak came
through the curtains,
she tried
to remove her mask.

It was then
that they both
agreed,
never to do that,
again.

Sinking Into Silence

It wasn't until just now,
after climaxing into
this blonde vegan's mouth,
and telling me that I made her cum
"like 10 times" with my hands,
as she lightly runs her fingernails down
my back, smiling into my chest
with such care and compassion,
that I realized

The woman I made into art,
gave my heart, my life, my artistic everything,

the one that now makes me walk down the street
with my hood over my head, headphones in,
my eyes sinking into the concrete
in hopes I don't see her,
that she was my
never attainable illusion.
A back unscratched.

Half Their Ages, Half My Soul

Went to the bar tonight
As I sip my beer
Watching three wives from Westchester.
Engagement and wedding rings
Shining brighter than the fluorescent lights of the bar
Huddled up with 3 bros half their ages
Laughing, flirting, touching, hugging,
Pecking on the neck
This is love, this is marriage
This is it?
I'm so tired of fighting.

Black Thong, White Lies

The Siren from Sardinia
Speaking to me in Italian
Io sono una donna sposata
Telling me about running
kilos of cocaine from
Italy to South America
Bringing back coke
on the plane in her vagina
she's reformed now
perfect American housewife and mother
she cooks me three meals for the week
before leaning over into the open refrigerator,

pulling down her black tights
black thong, black hair in my hands
reaching around and
rubbing the front of my pants
I look down and I see her
Not the Siren
But Her
The One That isn't Her.

The Second and Second to Last

The second and second to last people
he told about his abuse
was in a mandated NA meeting in Hampton, VA,
when he was 18, to explain to the room
what brought him to using drugs and alcohol.

As the story of the pit unfolded,
the heroin, crack, meth addicts
looked on horrified,
and no one talked to him after the meeting.
He smoked a cigarette to make sure.

He stopped going until
15 years later,
after drinking all night,
manically spending
hundreds at the casino,
rawdogging a 5-foot-nothing
girl with dreads on the floor
of his messy 1 bedroom apartment.

He woke up the next day,
went to an AA meeting in New York.
No one talked to him after the meeting.
He smoked a cigarette to make sure.

The Awakening

Three drinks in,
and you can stave off the thoughts
that make you not one of them.

Six drinks deep,
and you are the epicenter
a grand narcissistic epidemic.
But you don't know.
Not yet. Too many beers deep.

Not until the hungover awakening,
when the sun burns you in your bed
or theirs.
When regret cracks on your lips,
dry as the juices flaking
from your unprotected dick,
sticking to stained sheets
like a bad decision you swore
you'd never make again.

And then,
you forget.

And do it all again.

The Man in Black:
Reasons to Become an Artist

The first weekend he arrived in New York,
he got on an app and found a red-headed girl from Brooklyn.
She was rich, lived in the city for a while,
family in Connecticut, and liked the artsy types.
She drove back early from a ski resort in Vermont,
pretty excited to meet him.

"You seem different," she said.

After he finished painting a piece,
one he probably ended up setting on fire
in some bipolar II depression,
an abstract surreal figurative
hashtag contemporary
neo-expressionist oil on canvas
filled with a mix of ancient symbolism
and modern-day technological hyper-sexuality
that someone would need a theology degree
and a subscription to Pornhub to figure out.

They got drunk at an antique shop/bar fusion
and then came back to his place.

She looked down at his faded black jeans, broken zipper,
paint-chipped hands, and scraped black boots,
as he smoked a cigarette on his tattered screened-in balcony,
sitting on a rickety wooden bench
with the woodgrain face of an alien,
ranting about the cynicism of man,
the art of being human.

So fucking cliché for an alien in this place.

She looked at him with wide, admiring eyes and a big smile.
"You're what all the hipsters in Williamsburg
try to be, pretend to be. A real artist."

He laughed.
It gave him the polar opposite sensation of worthiness
that he thought she intended.

"Imitation is the highest form of flattery," she said.
He just replied,
"Good for them.
I hope it gets them laid."

It was 3 a.m., and they headed inside.
He put on a Johnny Cash vinyl record,
and she blew him in his living room.

When they woke up,
she cooked him curry.

Another reason he became an artist.

He Listened to "Livin' in Exile"

I wish I noticed his pain,
But I was in my own.
I was with him
In that car, blaring the song,
I felt it.
It connected with us.
I wish I listened to the lyrics for him, not me.
Fuck.
I wish I could have shown him love,
I thought I did.
Enough.

He wore *Wasted Youth* t-shirts,
I thought it was the hardcore punk scene.
I wish I saved him.
Now his son has no father.
Fuck.

If you'd never been there,
You'd never understand.
I wish I didn't have to escape
My life. I could've saved him.
His son could've had his daddy.
Fuck.

Why did I have to be so obsessed with getting out?
Fuck.
Fuck, fuck.
I miss you, Bobby.
I miss you so much.
I fucked up, I'm so sorry.

I got drunk once, remembering Bobby,
An Italian girl in my bed, daddy owned
A pizza shop in New York.
I was so angry at losing him,
When I could have saved him.
I blared the song loud,
As she fell asleep.
I'm a piece of shit,
I deserve the outcome.
She left.
I understand.
They all fucking leave.
I'm going back down South.
I need to save myself.

Escape from New York

He decided to leave it all behind,
New York City, for good,
in the rotunda of Penn Station,
Dunkin' Donuts coffee in hand,
watching the chaos of the masses
next to Hudson News.
Sarah Jessica Parker rushed through,
handlers trailing like shadows,
once the common folk were swallowed whole,
vanished without a trace.

The unmedicated schizophrenic
shook him from his early morning haze,

asking for a donation for his 'plan.'
He offered food
but the man just stared,
mumbled, and stumbled away,
calling him a 'motherfucking alien bitch,'
before climbing into a trashcan,
fishing out a half-eaten black and white cookie,
knocking the fast food wrapper
against the metal ring,
tucking it into his tattered jacket pocket.

He walked over to the ticket window,
oversized backpack slung over his shoulder,
past assault rifles and bomb-sniffing canines,
spending a few extra bucks
to upgrade to business class.
Not much difference,
Amtrak's always acceptable on the cheap,
but the last car was away from the people
he was over them,
all of them, himself included.

For the extra legroom,
and the refreshment cart,
he took a ten-dollar beer to the head,
settling in the first row by the window,
earphones in, pushing play,
grabbing his journal.
"Don't Think Twice, It's Alright,"
Waylon Jennings on repeat.
The reflection of overhead lights
bounced off the blackened window
and back into his face,
just another artist
who came for something
and left with something else.

"Failure has many forms," he scribbled,

feeling it more than understanding it.
Not because he didn't realize parts of his dream,
but failure felt like failing to realize
the depths of it all.
That emptiness,
still haunting him like the rats
scurrying in the dirty, dark Manhattan underground,
rattling beneath the train.

His art hung in galleries
Soho, Los Angeles, Seattle,
a magazine once offered representation
for a price.
The show openings, the groupies,
the worthless kid inside thought that was the answer.
Validation through recognition, sex,
the life of a real artist.
But it wasn't,
the story still untold.

The train jolted forward, not back to the South,
Not yet, he's headed upstate, to the north country,
to experience the reality of everything of today
and his past.
In retrospect,
he wasn't sure what he was thinking,
going upstate.
Misguided attempts at filling a pit
that was never meant to be filled,
a hope that could never be realized.

An abandoned boy running after his father,
who moved up north when he retired.
The train exited the tunnel,
passing Midtown, Upper West Side, Harlem,
the Hudson River line.
The city passed by him,
no longer hypnotizing,

no longer pumping life into his veins.
No longer vibrated with creative inspiration.
The art's done,
the drunken nights blacked out,
the shows a blur,
the food digested,
the women validated.
Desensitized by the reality.

Walking the busiest streets,
once felt like walking through a dream,
the land of Oz
something better than him,
a place for those with more talent,
more money,
more attractive qualities.
He thought if he could get there,
maybe all this suffering would be worth it.
Maybe he'd be worth it.
But when he finally made it,
all he found was trash,
on the curb, in the galleries.
Art openings were for the rich,
the privileged
no one from his background,
no one who fought for escape.

He fought himself out of Virginia
to chase this New York artist dream,
a delusion of grandeur he'd developed,
a place to find worth in his struggle.
His gifts of expression born from trauma.
His mom had called it,
a *delusion of bipolar grandeur.*
Maybe she was right.

As a survival tactic,
sitting in a small, dirty room,

his sister gone,
his mom gone,
his dad never there
he clung to dreams
or he would have become a statistic.
He'd die in spirit and form.
He looked to those who got out:
Iverson, Vick, Pharrell, Timbaland.
He tried out for teams,
made beats,
turned poetry into rhymes.
Selling CDs at bowling alleys,
scribbling poetry in his smoky car,
searching for a way out.

But eventually, opportunity dried up.
No talent, nowhere to go.
It wasn't until later,
back in school,
he took an art history class from Joe.
Joe was from New York,
a real art expert, he got it
and the first guy to ask him questions about himself.
He showed him contemporary art,
mid-century modern,
abstract expressionism.
Joe helped him craft his thesis
on Jungian psychology and Jackson Pollock.
He still teaches it today.

He stayed in touch with Joe over the years,
but no one ever responded to his novel.
Not Joe, not the publishers,
not anyone.

And now, as he heads Upstate,
he leaves that delusion behind,
to chase another one,

a father.
He might get off in Albany
and head back down South.

The South Don't Bury Its Dead:
A Return to Ruin

Dirty Little Secret

she mounts me in the backseat
of a jacked-up red dodge truck, 2008,
dyed purple and blonde hair, one nipple ring,
the other lost somewhere, maybe miles back.

baby seat to my left,
white country rap pulsing
through the speakers and her pussy.
she whispers,
"i love being your dirty little secret,"
as her husband drives us around
this forgotten southern town,
shadows of the old wars watching.

she moves, labia sliding over me,
her husband shifts gears,
she's begging me to go deeper
until they drop me off at my place.

"come meet us next week,
we'll do it again," she says.
she was tight, surprisingly so,
like, really surprising
for a gangbang girl.

Glass Reflection

Saw myself in the storefront glass,
a twice-dead man,
a hollowed-out shell,
some ghost of a past self
who never made it past the dreaming.

Alone on the balcony,
nothing left but graves of ambition,

ghost towns of what-could've-beens,
and a sky that don't care if I jump.

Fuck it all.

Don't look back in anger, no,
look back in surrender.
I gave up my dreams
or they gave up on me,
dragging me down like cement shoes
in an East River that never knew my name.

Maybe they were the kind of dreams
that bury you alive.
Maybe I was born in that dirt,
meant to die in it.
Meant to stay underground,
digging at the roots of something
that was never gonna grow.

The South Don't Bury Its Dead

The farmhouse porches
sag into the ground,
old trucks rust down
to their oxidized bones.

Everywhere he looks,
something down here is dying slow.
The South don't bury its dead,
it lets them sit out in the sun,
for everyone to watch them decompose.

He drives around just to be near them,
boarded-up windows,
walking dead with no expectations,
no hunger for success, no need to impress.

He can breathe again.

No one wants anything from him.
He can be a failure,
sit out in the Southern sun,
and rot.

A Priestess of the Southern Gods

She places a symbol over her tits
before every sin,
She sips her wine like
it's of holy blood sacrifice,
She snorts the powder and
swallows whole
like its flesh of the gods.
He watches her survive,
wondering if her gods
are the same ones
that stopped believing in him.

Look at Me Like Smoke

Look at me
the way you look at
a half-burnt joint,
sparking back to life,
a second chance at euphoria
before the inevitable end.

Blue heelers and bloodhounds
howl in the backyard,
calling something older
than domestication.
Two broods of cicadas,

three separate rings,
a choir of the damned

It all starts with a beer, a hit,
the hope I can keep writing.
I have to.
But why?

Kennedy pins on punk jackets,
blue and white,
once irony, now prophecy.
Bobby's son bends the knee to Trump,
and the masses march blind
because it was written,
because it was always written.

Twitter/X vomits into our mouths,
feeds us only what we want,
never what we need.
We rot from the inside out.

Discourse is dead,
buried beside the American dream.
But even corpses deserve a rebuttal.

The Russians have their side.
The Ukrainians draw their lines.
And war is razing the Holy Land,
the smoke smells the same
no matter where it burns,
Even here from old furniture factories.

But here I sit,
as my hound stares at me,
ears like satellite dishes,
eyes of honeyed glass,
one paw lifted,
a wild thing made tame,

a coyote disguised as a dog.

I see myself in him,
half-wild, half-domesticated,
howling at a world
only wanting a treat
And a pat on the head.

Trust the Process:
One Night in Georgia

The drunk girl with the blue hair,
tie-dye psychedelic mushroom bag,
won't shut the fuck up.
He interrupts her and says,
"Nice hair."
She gives him a shocked look,
curling her lip up.
He realizes it's a wig
and drinks some more.

He's been a Southern man,
drinking Virginia whiskey
in New York bars so long
he hardly remembers
how to be a drunk,
drinking New York beer
in a Southern bar.

The DJ has his setup,
spinning records
for these three drunks
in a cramped tavern
in Georgia.
You can tell the music,
it's his whole life.

Figuring Southern hospitality,
he gets up from his stool,
after hearing a hint of soul,
politely asks the DJ,
"Do you have the Bobby Bland,
Dreamer album?"

The DJ snaps back,
"Trust the process, man."

He appreciates the passion on some level,
but the narcissism reeks off his breath.
He's playing mashups of 1980s
and 2000s pop music.
At least be obscure in the set,
he thinks.
That way, he can tell himself that
you're cooler than him.
A skill he learned in Williamsburg.
Brooklyn, not Virginia.

The DJ throws on two records
And the violins of
The Thong Song
mixed with the vocal intro of
Cash Rules Everything Around Me.

He laughs, remembering running
into Sisqo at the train station in Richmond,
And then flashes of memories, getting punched,
in the back of the head repeatedly
at a Wu-Tang Clan concert in '97.
Hampton University.

For clarity, he did punch the guy back,
but almost got murdered for his
unconscious reaction
on the arena floor.

He had to fight his way out of that one.
A skill he learned in Virginia,
not New York.

He drinks some more.

A sad bridal party of three enter
from the border of North Carolina
and Virginia, western part of the state,
not where he's from.
They post up next to him,
moving their upper bodies to the music,
stuck on their seats.

Maybe he should have trusted the process,
he thought.

He finishes his drink, pays the bartender,
and heads outside to smoke a cigarette.

The bride follows him out,
asks him to light hers,
then asks if he wants to share a joint.

He does.

He points to her wedding veil,
and sash that reads 'Bride to Be,'
drunkenly, he asks,
"Do you trust your process?"

She pulls the pot out of her purse.

"I trust God.
Do you believe in God?"

He says,
"I might believe in God,

but I don't believe in trust."

They share the smoke.

He tells her,
"I'm going to his house.
I'll tell him about you."

He tries his luck, and ambles down
the dicey road, sitting himself
on the sidewalk, deathly
leaning against a live oak,
under the nose of the warm illumination
emitting from the stained glass
of the Church of Saint Philip,
smokes another cigarette,
taking a few pictures on his phone,
and asks God if He sees him.

He drags his self away in silence.
Question unanswered.

Middle School Memories and Middle-Aged Choices

OJ Simpson died today.

It was a middle school dance,
When the white Ford Bronco
Was running from the cops.
He was with some kid named Skip
In his mom's bedroom,
Watching the chase,
While she laid on the made bed
In awe.

They eventually left for the dance.

He made out with Shelly,
On the top of the dark bleachers,
Tongue for the first time,
He was proud of that.

Grunge kids sat cross-legged in front
Of the smoke machine and strobe lights.
They snorted pixie sticks in the bathroom,
Said it got them high.

Now, all these years later,
A married woman in
A Tennessee trailer park wants him.
Wants him to drive 90 miles,
Across the forest,
Across state lines.
Do some coke and
"Make her pussy his."
Her son's asleep,
Her husband's working out of town,
He doesn't need to know, she says.
She's listening to Kanye West,
After the cancel.

She wants to wear the ring
While grabbing his dick.
Welcome to marriage.
Good luck to you,
And your choices.
He'll just stay quiet.
He's been keeping secrets forever.

Howls from the Double Wide

Why do all these trailer park women
have some representation
of a coyote or wolf on their bedroom walls?

Each one of them,
from the growlin' screen, a flame of tinder,
into the light of a howlin' moon,
a hangin' Native American tapestry
in the upper left-hand side
of the poster print or velvet painting,
or maybe a statuette of the canine
on the nightstand.
Next to the condoms.

You can run free in this trailer park.
The native reservation is just across the field:
She's here with a sex addiction
and a few bucks for the casino.

Let's fucking go.

Sex without a condom.

Devouring Karma

I never believed in forever love,
not since the fifth time
it kicked me in the dick,
split my lip,
and left me laying.
Bitterness on my tongue,
lemon juice in the eyes,
resentment poured straight up,
stretching to the end of this bar.

So when you drink,
if the universe rips love from your hands,
take it back.
Don't roll over.
Get drunk.

Wreck a marriage
with a six-pack of beer and bad intentions.
Better if they have kids,
because the universe doesn't care for you,
or them bastard kids,
or their bedtime prayers.
I know.
I was one of them.

If you're going to do it,
do it right.
Find yourself a Southern belle,
yellow teeth, yellow dress,
still cooking the same Sunday dinners,
trapped in the same town,
the same man,
the same what-ifs.

Or make it an Italian import,
a Manhattan wife sculpted
for social media follows,
six-pack abs and a diamond band,
whispering sins in broken English
between doggystyle and tummy time.

Because they say the world
doesn't owe you a damn thing.
And if that's true,
then nothing means shit.
And if it's eye for an eye,
then rob the bastard blind.

If karma exists,
I've swallowed it whole.

So cook me the collards,
pour the sweet tea,
leave the porch light on for your husband,

and don't take your ring off.
Let me taste your safe choices.

"Can an evil man be brave?"

"Can an evil man be brave?"
She asked once over a fire,
beer in one hand,
cigarette in the other.
He didn't answer.
Some questions
ain't meant to be answered.
Not this day and age.

Recalling Your Memory

You're like driving alone,
Late at Night.
Down an unlit back road,
sheets of heavy rain.
Like the ones in Southeastern Virginia,
trees both sides of me, scream at me,
as every window is open, surround me.

One thousand pointed
Cimmerian deer
Bolt and Dart out
Ahead of me.

Every aphotic eye rebounding,
Lucid halogen dream, beamed.
Laying bare a smoke,
Trailing up your cheek, steam.
The washing of an apparition of you,
In the passenger's seat.

Monochrome embers,
pulsate in cadence.
With entire revolutions,
Veering and skidding
into abdominal walls. Vacant.

Dried ink on the seat,
Cracked paint on the wheel.
Parked driveway,
laid out in defeat.
Laid out on your shield.
And that ends the story,
of you and me
Laid out at your feet.
Just You and Me.

His Life's Purpose

Get drunk.
Find people.
Play with boundaries,
a slow-build crescendo
into the kinky dark.

Get home later than two.
Take a shower.
Write.
Beat off,
go to bed listening to YouTube,
Phil Collins' *Invisible Touch* live.
No autotune, that's talent.

Headed to Charlotte tomorrow
to watch Ecuadorian brothers play guitar.
Russia's still in Ukraine,
you can watch the killings on X.
The president can't remember names,

and Trump is on the rise again.

"Now I know
she's got a built-in ability
to take everything she sees.
And now it seems
I'm falling, falling for her."

Cum

A latent Catholic guilt
creeping into the corners of his mind.

A fight against,
fuck that,
he had fun.
Life is good.

He smells smoke,
thinks the factory here
burns things at night,
hidden from sight,
killing Southerners
before they even know it.

Done Dirty Down South

When the Reaper comes knockin',
don't bother cleaning your house
or getting your fine china, given to you
by your granmama.
Don't cover the beer rings stained
on the table your granddaddy gave you.
Don't smile and don't answer the door.

Just kill the lights,
slide under the bed,

and pray the bastard don't smell the piss
soaking your jeans.

All you need to do is take one more shot,
start thinkin' real hard
'bout what you gonna tell Jesus
when he asks about that naked stripper
who robbed you in that nasty motel
down in Dixie.

Gone Fishin'

She's got whiskey-colored eyes,
a shotgun on the wall behind her,
and a way of smiling
with her bottom yellowed teeth
that makes decent men want to
throw away their lives.

The hopeful lay their money down,
dangle their net-worth,
like bait in their nets.

She takes it, the bait,
but not their fate,
and they go home,
to their pregnant wives.

A New Life for $25

A woman offered him a new life.
She moved down south with her son,
escaping a fourteen-buck-an-hour grind.
Now she's just started at McDonald's.

She used to strip in New Hampshire,
but now she sends him a picture of her one-year-old.
Says the kid gets attached quickly.

Today, she had child support court.
She gets ninety-nine bucks a week
but needs him to Cash App her twenty-five
for some wine.

Her sister's about to kick her out.
She's asking for his Bitcoin now,
says it's for a bus ride back home.
Cheaper than flying.
He says 'naw.'
She disappears.

Thailand, North Carolina

hung over
blinking *thai food* door sign hung over
first customer since it opened at 4:30,
she told him with a smile,
neon *boba* light humming soft,
a *visit thailand* poster hung crooked,

"what if God was one of us?"
playing low through the speakers,
soft as a prayer,
while next door,
they're selling tickets to the rodeo.

Five Fifty-Five

She worked at Lowe's,
six-foot-something, red hair,
555 tattooed on her neck, big tits, big belly,

scanning my bags of mulch,
hands moving quick,
fingernails chipped from too many customer
requests for large items from tall places.

Her words spit out uncontrollably,
her neighbor chained a dog to a tree,
She adopted the dog.
She killed a snake wrapped around
her front doorknob,
yellow teeth flashing a brave smile.

Vodka bottle waiting for her,
she says,
Thursday's her weekend.
"Come over later if you want," she says,
her voice low, pulling him in.
He says he can't, he's got to work tomorrow.
"but it's my Friday."

And he can almost smell the trailer,
hear the shuffle of bare feet
across creaky floors.

The heat of too much freedom
and too much time to get himself in trouble.

She smiles,
climbs onto the back of the cart
and rides out the door.

43 Degrees in a Nowhere Town

Walking home in a emptied out town, NC,
11:07 on a brisk 43-degree night.
Black leather jacket, bought cheap
at some mall in Hampton or Newport News,

back when I was 19,
when that shit was new
before Gen Z called it vintage.

Auntie Anne's, a flirt with the blonde
behind the counter,
then slip into the backroom of sneaker store
and drop five bucks on an unreleased Nas album.
Shit was blank. The only blank one.
All the rest,
words scratched into plastic,
but that one?
A ghost.
Art promised,
Never delivered,

She wants to talk now.
High, rambling about a threesome.
The bartender thinks maybe she'd go for sushi.
I don't know,
she hasn't sexted back yet,
probably won't.
So I speed walk,
dodging the walking dead and cartel lookouts,
ghosts and watchers,
shadows and questions.

I'm on a wicker couch now,
slight wind on the porch,
like a massage on my back.

dogs barking in the distance,
Shadow person moving just past the trees.
I hear a sound.

I want to make art.
I have to go in now.
I'll wait

but I don't think she's here.

I love her,
but she fucking punches me.
What would you do, motherfucker?

The Game She Plays

"Who was that? Your other bitch?"
She doesn't care about the answer.
She just wants to make him flinch.

Coyotes of Hell

After the shot,
they don't bark,
don't growl,
don't sing,
just wakened,
waiting for him
to make a
motherfuckin' move.

Fryin' Pan Philosophy

Pork belly sizzlin',
hot grease a poppin',
words heavier than cast iron.
A man talkin' about his past
while a woman is talkin' about their future.

"You wanna die, die.
You wanna live, live.
But quit sittin'

at the kitchen table,
Like you're at the
damn crossroads
talkin' like a philosopher
who ain't got the balls
to make a choice.
*Philosophers talk
Men act.*"

She don't serve pity.
Not for breakfast,
not for any man.
Definitely not any for pussies
wanting to be *her* man.

New Napoleon

I ate at a smokehouse and had a steak,
collards on the side.
The waitress had a cute lisp, a cute ass,
and toothpick legs holding up
her American dreams.
I tipped her 22 percent for the inspiration,
grabbed a slice of red velvet for later,
then hit the gas station
on the corner of a two-lane road,
the kind with no windows,
where the cigarettes cost more
than the place is worth.

Red hair outside,
a homeless man smoking his,
dragging on, as long as the day.
I grab a pack and a drink.

The foil peels back easy now,
not like before.

Used to be, you had to work for it,
pull the tab, rip it raw.
Now it slides open smooth,
an Apple product
for those who can't afford Apple products.

The first inhale is all it takes.
Menthol sting on my lips,
tobacco bite on my tongue,
that familiar yellow circle of the filter
A nicotine target forming a target
the whisper:

Let's fucking cause trouble tonight.

I head back to a bar
I swore off a year ago,
back when I fucked that swinger couple
and spent the next six months
dodging them around town.

But I'm tired of avoiding.
Napoleon walked back to Elba
without a shot fired.
I walk back in with my head high,
same intent.

This doesn't involve Louis XVIII.
Just a gangbang girl,
a judgmental Bible Belt town,
and some drunken vulnerability.

The moon hangs behind the kudzu tree,
suffocating it slow,
hollowing it out.
Invasive.

A hound dog scratches at the porch door,

wants out,
but I don't want him in this war.
This is a war council of one.
I'm about to take France back,
in the form of a broken-down town
in western North Carolina.

I push the doors open.
No one here.
Fuck. No one to conquer.
I order a beer one minute to close,
drain it, then walk next door.

The bartender is scrolling,
group texts flying in.
A picture of her tits,
her mouth on some other guy's dick.
No smile towards me.

I don't need a menu,
just another beer.
Two guys in the corner debate
women's basketball,
say they should put them in bikinis.
Oh shit. They're here.

Eye contact.
No contact.
I ain't surrendering.

No one looks at me.
No one speaks.
I walk through them like I own the place.
Cowards.
Talking about me,
but not to me.

I step outside,

light another cigarette,
wait.

She finally does.
We talk.
They slowed down, she says.
No more gangbangs.
I nod. I understand.

They take me home in their new car,
drop me off at the same spot
she left me last time,
climbing off my dick.

We are friends now, I think.
I'll see her next Thursday.
She gives me a hug.

I walk through my door
like an Appalachian Arc de Triomphe,
my old boots hitting the floor,
a conquering hero of doubts
and insecurities.

No shot fired to their face.
No money shot to their face either.
Maybe that makes me
a new Napoleon.

It's the Dogs That Still Haunt Me

Go With Him

He would paint her galaxies
and the heavens.
He would write to her of universes
and totality,
so that she would never have to
traverse that path,
never have to tread
into that murky bar,
never have to wake up
next to that vaporous stranger.

He would carry the universal truths
she'd never have to confront.
He'd let her live and breathe through him,
to look down at her demise,
while looking up at her prize.
To take his hand,
he promised her:
he would return her to him,
so she'd never have to.

She'd never have to lie
in those four concrete walls,
never on that one cold metal bench.
She'd never have to be stalked or chased,
her heart drumming, hammering down,
like his typewriter.

She'd never have to pass out
on her terrain,
never have to relinquish
what she clutched closest.
He whispered again:

"Come with me.
You will be returned home."

The Last Mass

As a teenager
he bagged groceries and stocked shelves.
She was a cashier, full of life,
A pure soul, you know those types where you look
in their eyes and life hasn't fucked with them much,
Just his type, shorter than him, made him feel more like a man,
When his male ego was a bullshit facade.

Energetic, full of life, always smiling,
Kind to everyone, made him feel seen,
When no one made him feel seen.

Asked for a date,
She invited him to family dinner.
She'd recently broken up
With the chubby guy,
Gave him hope.
Said she didn't like smokers,
Or drinkers or weed smokers.
He stopped.

She wanted a Catholic man.
Which always felt out of place
in a city with a Baptist church
on every corner but he went.
He met her at church
every Sunday for a month,
Sat in the front row
with her and her family,
Stayed after mass to
fellowship with the congregation.
After the *sign of peace* one Sunday,
The priest whispered to the young man
To visit him in his office
 in the rectory sometime,
With an off smile.

After the service that day,
She told him she didn't want to date him,
She was getting back with the chubby guy
She said "but God bless you," gave him a big smile and hug.

Went home, got high, and beat off.
He never went back to church again.
He wonders sometimes,
If he had paid a visit to
Father Mike alone
in that empty building,
or if she had chosen him,
Where his soul would be at today.

If You're Not on the Horse

He swears to God, just hurt him.
Apathy over trauma is the coward's choice.
Pain, vices, love, and adrenaline,
the four pillars of being alive, being human.
Also, the same four horsemen of his apocalypse.

What other roads to death exist?
Apocalypses are only cruel
if you're not the one riding on the horse.

"Come here."

They Ain't Dyin' for You

friends, family, they ain't dyin' for you,
not like they used to, not like they claimed.
it's a story of growin' up,
of what friendship really meant
back when we knew,

we'd die for each other.

guns everywhere,
you trust 'em with your life,
9mm glocks, front seat,
cold steel, trust in the silence.
point to the bodies,
toss hands outside the tinted windows,
lights flashin', blue and red,
get the fuck out the car,
maybe this is where it all ends.

a felony traffic stop,
hands shaking,
the order's set,
ride
lights
intercom,
"hands, keys, toss 'em."
get out.
left shuffle,
knees hit the pavement,
service weapon behind your head.
don't fucking move,
don't fucking move.

boots crunchin' after rain,
shaky, sticky summer nights,
slammed face-first onto the ground,
the jerk of your shoulder back
and the reality sets in:
they ain't dyin' for you.

Feelings Fade, Orgasms Echo

Life is like meeting a beautiful woman,
Dancing with her all night,

Lips on your lips,
Going drink for drink.

Nurturing the flame,
The spark of this connection,
Unconceivable possibilities.

During the night,
You meet up with your closest friends,
And they love her.
You party all night downtown,
Celebrating this moment you've been waiting for.

Until your feet hurt from dancing,
And your cheeks hurt from smiling.
You hail a taxi cab back to your friend's place,
And they head to bed, happy for you two.

After she sucks your dick a little bit,
She says, "Let's not rush into this.
Let's not let it just become a physical thing."

There's a future here.
There's hope.
This is fate.
She is the one.
She is your future.
You just know you both feel it.

You pass out drunk, asleep on their couch,
In each other's arms.

Until you hear the moans of her pleasure,
As your best friend and her boyfriend
Fuck your beautiful woman
In their bedroom,
Until 5 a.m.

You're too drunk to leave,
So you smoke a cigarette
Until you sober up.

Then you have a hangover.
But hey, at least you didn't have to drive her home.

Mile Marker

A smile lasts a mile
in this path of least resistance.
You look down at night,
up there right above me,
The clock bell sounds,
it's time to lie to me
and tell me that you love me.

Spit Me into the Dirt

We are the forbidden fruits they write about.
Just do me this one favor,
after you consume me,
Spit the seeds back into the dirt,
don't bury me inside you.
Let the earth decide
if we can grow from this.

What She Remembers

He used to be the man
who'd bleed for her.
Now he's the man
who watches other people do it.

The One You Gave Away

She was the
smoky bell atop
A two-way mirror.
Ring, Run.
And it becomes
clear, clearer.
From You,
she revealed
An Inside Track.
Now she's A
Golden
Wedding
Bell.
Inside, Black.

Right Click

Listening to this song on a loop,
laptop slipping down my stomach
as I bring it back to my heart,
spilt beer droplets carried
by the curls of my chest hair,
thinking of you.

Waiting for you to walk through the door
even though you don't know where I live.

Every line hoping it hits you in your sleep,
but I never pick up the phone to say,
I hope life treats you kind.

I can't shake this hope,
that the universe sends you this message,
just listen, it's in the quiet.
My tears fall for no one but you.

I'll sleep on this couch,
waiting for you to find your way back.

Rock Bottom has Your Face

A good way to
know how ugly you are
is to gauge the guys
she posts on her social media
she has lower standards
than you think
And he's the upgrade.

clean shaven for the soul

i shave my beard off
so i can be the ugly
held behind
punishment for my sins
of lust and insecure vanity
a way to keep people away from me
or me away from people

i shave my beard
to let the ugly breathe,
no more hiding behind the lie
that i'm worth your time

like a dog snarling
behind a busted-out fence
cross the street and walk away

Love is just a Firm Grip

Soundless threats
on the sectional couch.
On the edge of the ledge.

One wrong exchange,
and she is out the door.
She's had enough of your shit.
And you've had enough of your shit,
But you can't help yourself.

You are infinitely flawed.

But you never give up,
because you love like no other.
In retrospect, she was just the tightest you had
and she opens the door.

In that second,
you take her from behind
and bend her over.
You grab her hair.

She smiles.
She welcomes you.
And you're back.
You've reset
the clock til
Y'all implode again.

Grasping Smoke

Last Night

He dreamt the perfect words,
better than anything

he could ever write.
He felt the warmth
as he slept,
the synchronicity
of every line,
bare against his breath.

He woke, grasping
for the words
to write down
and immortalize,
only to feel them
dissolve at his touch.

It was a gift,
from his subconscious,
or the universe,
or God.
A fleeting reminder
to never possess
perfection,
to never clutch
the unreachable.

The splendor
of exasperated hope.

A Bed Burns with Consequences

She hits him in the chest,
Then the face
scratches his cheek and neck,
curses him for even thinking about leaving,

They fuck like war.

Like his punishment.

Like her prayer.

Take it Back

To the keepers of the heart:
Do not run but
Do not walk.
into any sanctuary during the flood.
Rise with your hands held firm.
Be front and
be centered.
Conscious and brace yourself.
She will be watching.

As it's our actions,
that delineate us, as
The truest word ever spoken
can just as easily be wiped away
with another word said.
But a corrupt action,
can never be
justly retracted,
by another
faithful action.

to this, remember.
the keepers of the heart.

No More

It has turned on him.
He is no longer that man.
This should be it for him.
He's afraid it won't be.

He hopes it is.

So he pops that pill,
sips that drink,
rips that feel,
sinks that ship.

Deep sleep,
into the great flood.
A drunken dream
overtaking the SUV.
He is drifted out to sea,
never to be seen.

Rush around.
Enter the bedroom.
Select the game.
Press start on the
television screen.

Transported,
looking up into the stands,
he sees the boy, smiling.
One face
in a sea of faces.

No longer lost at sea,
and no one ever died,
because no one ever dies.
They press the button and
they start over.

In the Shape of Bullets

As a child, he used to hear voices, kind of.
Maybe it was the traumatic brain injury,
maybe the trauma,

maybe just the brain itself,
or maybe all the emotional injuries combined.

But it wasn't like a clear voice,
more like whispers
hidden in the static of a television.
Something different
than the usual inner dialogue,
the day-to-day voice in his head.

Eventually, the static left.
The whispers stopped completely
after he turned 10 or 11.
They didn't come back much after that.
But sometimes,
they would.

Like when he walked down the road alone
or sat at the kitchen table,
biting into baby carrots,
shaping them into bullets with his teeth.

He'd wonder what those bullets
would feel like in his mouth
if they were real,
and fast.

Really fast.

Then maybe it would all be quiet.

G.A.G.

His father's wife,
God Awful Greada,
didn't soften for a child already
without a father.

If anything, she hardened.
Relying on extreme food punishment,
she seemed to get off
on his suffering during those
forced weekend visits.

She'd watch with delight
as he gagged,
tears pooling over a plate
of vomit-covered box-mashed potatoes.

It wasn't the flavor,
but the texture.
Gritty chunks like dirt clumps,
a sensory reminder of being buried alive.
The pale color, the color of, well, things,
as the mix turned cold.

He'd try to force it down his throat,
just to escape back to his room.

"You can't get up until you finish.
You're not leaving until it's all gone."

But life,
as he found,
is never finished.
And it's never all gone
And there's always
Laughing in the other room,
Loud enough for you to hear.

Music in Cars

Eleven years old, late at night,
his mother was driving them home

through a Sunday storm.
They had to get back for work and school.

He was half-asleep, listening in and out,
the hum of the highway
tires rotating, wipers wiping,
matching the rhythm of his heartbeat
as the weather worsened.

Blinking hard to stay awake for his mother,
he watched as the fog crawled
across the windows.

The interstate slick with storms,
snow falling heavy, headlights cutting
only a few feet through the darkness.

Then black ice caught them.

Spinning circles,
360 degrees, over and over,
10,000 Maniacs on the tape deck,
"Because the Night- Live"
screaming through the speakers.
He grabbed the door handle,
fingers slipping from the centripetal force
tossing him around the car.

A few revolutions later,
the car slammed to a stop,
jolting his head and neck forward,
the seatbelt squeezing a gasp
from his chest.

They bottomed out
on the Virginia pine forest floor,
the car completely totaled.
The smell of leaking oil,

burnt tires,
crushed metal,
and the song still plays:

"With doubt the vicious cycle turns, and burns."

The engine began to smoke.

Later, the highway patrolman said,
"This was the only opening for miles,
you're lucky, Son."

But the patrolman didn't know
what a lucky son was.

When he had to be with his father,
or rather, when his father was forced to be with him,
the man would play the music for the lucky son.

"Cat's in the Cradle" by Harry Chapin,
and a live version of
"A Boy Named Sue" by Johnny Cash.

Over and Over again.

His father laughed about it,
singing lyrics about horrible fathers.

"When you coming home, Dad?"
"I don't know when,
but we'll get together then."

Or,

"Son, this world is rough,
and if a man's gonna make it,
he's gotta be tough.
I knew I wouldn't be there

to help you along."

He didn't know
if his father was trying to toughen him up
or if he man was just a narcissistic sociopath.

old dogs and young men

when i was nine,
my father paid me fifty bucksto take the his dog in to die.

he handed me the leash,
told me to tell them i found her on the side of the road.
"cheaper than putting her down at the vet."
and i believed him.
believed him right up until
i walked back to the car,
fifty bucks in my pocket,
and a stomach full of something i couldn't name.
a price i couldn't pay

years later,
after the bars,
the backseat rides,
the women,
the drugs,
the ssris
the mood stabilizers
the betrayals,
the cage,
the long years grinding
my bones to the deaf,
i finally found the word for it.

murder

First Class to Heaven

He once watched his father
watch the news,
the Pope riding the streets
of some impoverished country,
waving from his luxury vehicle.

His father turned to his wife,
childlike wonder in his gaze,
eyes wide and shimmering,
like something out of a Disney movie.
"Wow," he said,
"he gets a first-class ticket to heaven."

He meant it.
Those doe eyes,
filled with astonishment,
like a child speaking of Santa.

And that's when it clicked.
Who he was dealing with.

He remembers
when that same man
beat him.

A Stigmata of Shame

After the car crash, he really started crashing out.

In school he'd fight, cuss, ignore the rules,
He was pissed at the world,
his father, his father's wife,
and his abusers he buried in his dissociated mind.

One last chance to turn it around,

turned into "You're kicked out."
He was dictated to move in with
his father and his abusive wife.

They forced him into a Catholic school for 6th grade,
the first day of his sentence,
they made him stand and get measured
for an appearance in the court of their public opinion
into thick polyester uniform pants.
Grabbing all over his junk.
Suffocation around the genitals.

When the school year started,
they scratched him all day,
and skin-tight sensory torture consumed him.
He'd squirm in his seat, a never-ending itch,
His groin tingling uncontrollably.
He'd bounce his leg all day, clenching his penis and ass,
trying to escape the anxiety
burning from the fabric between his legs.

The summer months made it worse.
Those pants, fucking him without consent
every fucking day.
All day, all he could think about was
the moment he could rip them off.
One day, he said to himself, fuck it,
he wasn't going to suffer anymore
in that 15 minute walk in the oppressive Virginia heat.
So he started packing baggy shorts in his book bag
and snuck them out of the house in the morning.

That day as soon as the school bus
dropped him off at his stop,
He ran into the thin strip of trees, a barrier,
between a neighborhood and the main street.
Nature's desperate changing room.

He'd change there for a few days,
a small rebellion from the outside,
but an urgent need of relief from inside.

During the day, his body screamed to get
out of those pants and away from his skin,
the buried abuse clawing at his mind,
trying to break through to make him remember,
his subconscious pushing it down,
too much for a brain to handle at 11 years old.

His father's wife came home early one afternoon
And saw him changing in the trees.
She mocked him endlessly,
called him gay, proclaiming that he wanted
the other boys to see his privates,
because he never had a girlfriend,
he must be a little gay boy.

Couldn't even keep his
shoelaces tied sometimes
to her precise specifications.
So she made him wear Velcro shoes
to school and to basketball practice for a year
At an age way past that being the norm.

Later that year, his punishments would escalate
in severity from verbal to physical.

The boy made a friend and that kid
brought a handgun to school.
He showed it to him in the bathroom once.
But no one ever found out about that,
he had condoms in there too,
A 11 year old with a black 9mm
and handful of blue Trojan condoms.

Later that week,

The friend called the boy
back in the bathroom
for another "show and tell."
This time, he and two of his henchmen
were giving some kid a 'Swirlie,'
jamming this kid's head in the toilet and flushing.

The boy left quickly,
He knew this wasn't going to end well,
And had been verbally beaten into compliance by that point,
So he wanted no part of that activity.
The piss haired kid locked eyes
with the boy as he was leaving.

About 30 minutes later, he got pulled out of class.
The head nun who happened to be the principal
immediately rang his father at work.
In that moment he knew shit was going to be bad,
but he didn't know what to expect exactly.

Back at his father's house, he awaited for
the sound of the garage door opening,
which was a sign one of them returned,
which was never a good thing.
The boy went to the door to get in front of it,
tell his innocent side of it all.

He tried his best to explain
to his father that he wasn't involved,
he wasn't there for all that,
he saw it but didn't participate.

He said he didn't fucking believe the boy
and it's no use to lie to him because
he's a human lie-detector.
He did tell him the truth
He said "Bullshit."
And told the boy to drop his pants

and bend over.

The boy slowly laid his upper body on
the stiff bed under him,
his body weight pressing into the flat mattress.
The embarrassment of his father
seeing his bare ass in the air.

He thought,
"My body feels too big for this."
Like they were both acting,
playing roles they aged out of,
no longer fit into.

But he was wrong.
His body hadn't outgrown beatings.
That feeling left him on the third or fourth
police-issued belt strike across his ass and back.

He beat that right out of him,
His Irish Catholic birthright,
engraved in leather.
Passed down from generations before him.

All the while,
those tight pants scratching up the boys ankles
for a crime he didn't commit.

Luckily, soon after,
the boy was exiled back to his mother's house
And in retrospect,
that boy would've taken that beating every day
if it meant escaping that house and those pants.

Palm Sunday

Hands open,
dripping of his holy water,
but never clean.

And he says it low,
like it's already written,
in the red dirt:
"Sons don't listen to their daddies,
do they?"

Only the silence stands between 'em,
and piles of banned books
recounting the fucked up history
of father and son,
burning like the library of Alexandria.
They will never be told,
unless the boy saves them.

No. 2 in the end

he pressed the No. 2 pencil to the page,
snapping the tip off
like a mountain wife in a chicken coop
like the last straw on a bad life,
like the fracture of his finger
ready to sacrifice limbs to the gods,
for words, for art.

graphite dust on his hands,
yellow paint flecks on his beard,
he took his tired words,
the last fight he had left,
and dragged his fingerpad
through the dust,
a dark gray smudge,

over and over until
a final fade to black.

when you don't have a pistol,
you have to use a pencil.
a pistol won't write a poem.
but it sure as hell can end one.

Hashtag Hyenas

He can't help but think
about the people
who claim to care for the
true bearers of the pain,
protesting in the street,
casting their vote,
placing a flag next to their
social media handle,
claiming they know the pain,
they are experiencing the pain.
They claim they feel the pain,
they're empaths
and they suffer too.

But when you're truly in need,
when you're truly hurt,
when this life has pissed on you,
left you suffering in a ditch
with no money,
no direction,
no guidance,
no help, nothing but the feeling
of true hopeless pain,
the moment you wake up,
you're just looking down
a barrel of a fucking gun,
called Death.

You couldn't even begin to worry
about the plight of others.
You could only think
of how to get through
this next second
without taking one step closer
to killing yourself.

So instead of making a post online
or a sign to wave for yourself,
go to the poorest part of your
town and give some kid a $50
and a way the fuck out.

EMPTY. FUCKING. SOUNDS.

empty. fucking. sounds.

we got too smart too fast,
but not smart enough to handle it.
we were meant to crawl through
the earth for sex, food, and water,
until we created war, developing
a need for the taste of blood.
now we crawl through the dirt
wearing suits,
writing checks,
praying to ghosts, and
making ghosts of any young man
who's land stands in our way,
or bank account.

nature don't give a damn and
she'll let you in on her secret
if you listen long enough.

none of this carries weight with her,
not the visions you carve in stone,
not the sins you try to wash away,
not the words you spit like venom
or swallow like dirt.

all just empty. fucking. sounds.

mammalian vibrations
we use to keep each other down,
or put a little sugar in the tea
before the knife slips in and stirs.

and when you apologize for the stab?
it's just more noise,
just more breath wasted on the wind.
you can't unring a bell.
you can't pull a bullet back from a heart,
and you can never put a bloody knife
back into a leather sheath.
it will rot the skin from the inside out.

the static in his head

monochrome madness flickers,
his broken mind
calls out through
the burnt-out tubes.
there ain't no signal,
it's not even hooked up here
just the kaaahhh of his own destruction,
just the sound of a life dissolvin'
into black and white snow.
it's a beautiful
black and white landscape.

Caustic Sea

Embrace that iron revolver
into my steel chest.
Allow your shadow,
neon red spiked nail
to tap and tap,
and tap
on that trigger.

Let your dust jacket
Obscure the outside view.
An elevation, the bend of your
flushed lips.
A gaze through your
impenetrable lashes.
I hate that,
you know you have me.
So flip, run,
your finger down my face,
and to my stomach.
Death was coming for dinner,
And you RSVPed.

Accompanied by Seventeen
hungry, ravenous hounds.
Follow thee procession.
As well as the next, X, Eleven.
Fourteen forty-four,
Never remembering the exact second,
Until the trembling,
Core.
As the time rises,
into the ground,
Seven, seven to the well,
Found.

Run to the floor,

Through the sliding door.
Weeps for Thou,
picturesque.

Oh, what a sound,
There it is, lies in the halls
of the southernmost library calls.
Well, we are here.
Together, separated.
Through the wall.
Pull back,
the hard cover falls.
For you, yes, the second
this second.
Memory for us, take this.
It is ours, second.
Never to be swiped from the back.
Pocket enters the fray of
seventeen, relax.
Hounds,
Twenty five, three, two, one.
This is it.
Four, and it is for us,
You cannot turn away,
from what we see.
It is only
It is the only
our only way.

So free,
Free yourself and
feel the slip.
And just let it slip.
Pull back your hand.
And release your grip.
Let them fly
To the ground.
And when they hit

And bounce, flip, and found.

To stand tall
and make your choice.
Whatever you decide
It won't matter much,
rejoice.

Because you left it up
to gravity
And gravity always wins.
Just like you.
So I ask you,
Have you ever felt alive?
I meant
Truly alive?
5 Alive?
5 senses reeling and revolving,
perpetual movement and falling.

Your fate driving,
into the brink of what
really matters.
Your matter,
you matter.
In black and white.
Drifting
across the caustic sea.
It would now seem,
I bleed for thee.
Waves cut me and crash me.
And now you see.
I bleed for thee.

So I bleed for thee.
So be with me.

Through the drought,

Drink with me.
And
When you're left to
crave that water and
what you desire,
play the tape
on repeat
and again
with artillery fire.

So rewind the tape
during cold winter nights
and ancient summer days.
Until ONE O'ONE
Fahrenheit,
ONE O' ONE,
Different ways.

Reach out and touch me,
reach out and touch,
reach out and touch,
reach out,
reach out,
and touch.
Me.

Don't walk away,
reach.
Don't turn,
don't turn around,
don't turn around on me.

Reach,
please reach,
please reach,
please reach out.
TO ME.
Reach.

Don't turn.
Reach out,
reach out,
to me.

The Pit from Virginia to China

When he was seven,
he would wake to an empty home,
weekday, weekend, it didn't matter.
The blur of it all.
People with broken childhoods understand:
the days don't exist, just the blur.

A deadbeat Irish cop of a father,
gone two years now,
chasing women.
A mother, God knows where,
working, surviving.
An older sister, far beyond memory,
living in denial,
might as well not have existed.

"Roll over, roll over,
and the little one says…"
His little body rolled out of bed,
a mattress on the floor,
no frame.
Through the mess he'd wander,
searching for someone,
anyone.
But there was never anyone home.

Knocks on the window.
Knocks on the door.
The 12-year-old neighbor boy,
"Hey, wanna play?"

He'd walk him an acre next door,
hand him a shovel too heavy to carry.
"We're digging to China,"
the boy would say.
A better world than this one.
And so, he dug.

When the shovel grew too heavy,
he slid into the pit,
used his hands.
The boy would call out to his brother,
older, much older:
"Hey, we almost to China!"

A bloodshot Virginia cardinal
flew overhead.
And then the brother,
red-eyed and mean,
arrived at the pit's edge.
"Boy, you ain't gonna find China down there, dumbass."
He'd look up and smile out of fear.

And then the dirt would rain down,
shovelfuls of earth,
pellets of clay and dust
scatter-shotting his face.
Funny, isn't it?
the more time you spend in the pit,
the more you learn the taste profiles,
of dirt, the layers of clay,
each with a different flavor.
You acquire it.
A crud connoisseur.

But the scared smile fades.
He'd beg them to stop,
and for a moment,
they would.

Until the earth rained down again,
burying him alive
in the pit to China.

The brothers would jump down into the pit
and push his face further in the dirt
as they ripped his pants off.
Whispering in his ear to lay there
or they would bury him alive,
And no one would find me.

He froze.
He learned to clench his teeth,
to never lick his lips,
the dirt would remind him where he was:
in the pit with them.

His soul would rise out of his body,
hovering above the pit
like the bloodshot cardinal in the sky.
When they were done,
if he had done well,
he was allowed to leave,
to climb out of the pit.

But if he squirmed,
if he struggled that day,
the dirt would rain down again,
a relentless storm,
and they would begin to bury him alive.

After the laughter faded,
they'd let him crawl out just enough
to put his clothes back on.
A kick to the back would send him
toward the half-broken wood
and barbed wire fence.
He'd climb through,

heading back home,
to the empty house.

Excuses formed in his mind for the dirt,
for the state of him,
if anyone ever came home,
if anyone even noticed.
But they didn't care,
not when he left in the morning,
not when he returned.

On overcast days,
or in the rain,
he learned that the pit was always waiting.

Some days the brothers
would take him to their barn,
where hay became a nativity scene
for his naivety.
No frankincense, no myrrh, no wise men,
just shit, sweat, tears, and cum.
That's when he looked to the night's sky
through the hay bale opening
and followed the star of undeniable truth.

Comply or Die.

Ejaculate them or be Suffocated by them.
But nothing more important than,
Life is not fair,
and God does not care.
Prayer is psychological warfare.

Everlasting hope
is bombed out of you
with every unanswered Amen.

So smile up from the pit,

get used to the shit.
China ain't down there, dumbass.

All there is,
is a very real hell.
And you can't cry.
Because of
what they told him in the pit,
"Tears don't come,
if you don't gag.

The Alchemy of Rejection

When you've been told NO
your whole life,
you possess it,
you carry it with you,
and it shames you,
and strangles you,
and subjugates you,
until you realize
that this is it.
This is your experience.

You become
that rejection.
You are given
two choices:
Die grasping that NO,
or give NO
a new meaning.

You carve it into your back
and walk through
the swarming streets
of gainsaying gazes
and shaking heads.

When you've
grown up in poverty,
and the only word
you know is NO,
you take that word
and break any rule,
any law, any command,
in half.
you own that damned word.

When you've been told
that you will never be anything,
and you fight,
and you hustle,
and drive into
that obscurity,
you come out with
that word
branded
on your back,
your very soul.

As you crawl through the fire,
you rise from the ground,
a burnt and bloody heap.
You pull the bullet
from your chest,
and you keep coming forward.

You own that word.
You have become NO.
And nothing will ever
stand in your way.
He believed that.
All the way to the end.

Last Poem

Bukowski
buried a bluebird
inside of his drunken heart

before the time I found myself
trapped inside a crumbling grave.
Deep.

Neon red Virginia cardinals
sang songs for me to sleep.
Then suddenly, still.

A laughing heart went still.
A laughing gull feather,
fell still, into my hand,
and a bad gray man buried me alive for that.

I held that feather tight.
But that day,
at seven years old,
when I looked up at the last shovel full of dirt
coming down on me,

I died. Alive.

Under the silent screaming
Southern soil.

And as the cardinal flew off into the pines,
so came the coastal coyotes from the tree line.
They come to gather and cower
and chatter and chew
at the bones left gnawed inside of me.

Tonight,
after a few drinks,

and a few fucks,
if you were ever to do me the honor
of laying your burnt, jaded ear
onto my chest,
& silencing your racing thoughts,

you may be able to hear 'em howl.

And it's beautiful.
Sometimes.

Other times,
cascading cries cut
through caverns of chipped-up canines.
Their forlorn wails and whimpers, mournful,
habit rouses me out of bed. 3 a.m.

They whine out for me to save them.
Is your ear still to my chest?
Did you hear that?

Listen.

They are awake, scratching to escape.
1,000,000 grains of hope in each breath.
Biting bit by bit,
bite by bite.

Until the scratches, the barks,
the digging their way out
turns into nothing more
than a muffled white noise in your ear,
on my heart,

like a seashell stolen from the York River.

It's comforting to know I'm not alone.
If you can't hear them, that's okay.

You are not alone.

You're never alone with me.

The world has become deaf to them too.
Scar tissue provides an elite soundproof of concept.

I care for the coyotes now.

I sit down with those damned dogs
and tell 'em
they're now my damned dogs.
My dearest dogs.

I say, **"Dogs, come lay with me.
And one day, I promise,
someone outside of me
will see your worth.
Then is when
you'll finally be able to rest."**

They come as called.
Curling up next to me, sweet-like,
broken eyes looking up
into this hopeful abyss.

I smile slightly, the best I can muster,
and try to give them hope.

Hope is the only thing that I found
that keeps them alive,
and they survive, barely.
For decades.
For lifetimes.

**"It's time to quiet down your yowling about.
I promise you all,
I will tell your story.**

And that will be our way out."

They want to escape me,
in order to create,
but eventually, over time
and dissociation,
I can hear them as I fall asleep,
behind my breath,
the subtle scratching sounds
of depleted desperation,
they come crashing down
in defeated resignation.

The dogs lose all hope
and silence themselves
into a low whimper in the shadows.

I get some sleep.

However, despite my valiant efforts,
I've learned,
when left in a dark environment,
hope's half-life decays into resentment
within a few days.

Then the dogs start up again.
But they submit.
And climb back into the depths.

The **perpetual burial of dreams.**

Those skinny beasts howl and they growl underground.
They scratch deep inside of me.
They huddle in a broken pile to stay warm.
But there's no room to run inside their clinical depression.

So they stay huddled up, all night,
never fully falling asleep,

barking and howling below the surface
until they make me let them out.

They come to my classically conditioned whistle
and rush up from their lairs of despair,
burrowing their muddied muzzles
deep into the keys and blank canvases.

They create beautifully raw scenes
of their coyote experience here on this earth.
Tales of emotional and physical survival
over the existentialist traumascape they were thrust into.

When I look, when I smile at what they bring me,
they rapidly wag their tails of mange
in a speck of a moment of joy.

Hope is slightly returned.

They all sit in a line and I proudly look down
at my dear misunderstood companions
in loving approval and say,

"A job well done."

Patting each of their little scruffy heads,
scratching 'em behind their ears.

I reach down to pet them softly.
I'm apologizing,
trying to hold back a tear.

"I'm sorry, but that's enough, my friends.
It's time to go home.
The world isn't ready for you."

I force them back into the shadows,
because I have to.

The friends, the lovers, and the lives I help save
never know that those hungry dogs suffer in there.
Ripping me up
from the inside out.
Leaving me weaker,
their claws dig me deeper.

With a smile.

They will outlive me through these pages written,
and you will hear them tonight,
and they chitter knowing it.

Each day, I offer them a chunk of me.
They take for themselves.

It's enough to put a man on his knees.

But I kneel for NO man.

Do you?

God help us if these coyotes ever escape
and find one loving home.

A place where this pain
doesn't equate to love.

Maybe in my mind,
we all could love in harmony.

I may never live to see that day,
but I know an ultimate truth . . .

**Sometimes heroes of men (and coyotes)
get left behind and forgotten.**

I have done my best to be their silenced voice.

But my voice too was lost
a long time ago
in those Virginia pines.

Note from the Author:

This is the final flare in the air
When you are lost at sea.
There's Almost a beauty in it
watching it disappear
Hope dying out in the sky
as the camera pans out
The view from above
as I become a dot
on the island
this is me carving
into the Carolina oak,
CROATOAN.

After a life dying for my art to reach someone,
it's time to bury the artist where I found him,
in that dug out earthen pit
where that boy was defiled, buried alive,
and climbed out of the red southern dirt
to tell his story into the silent echoes of obscurity.
I tried kid, I really did.
I gave my life to you,
I sacrificed myself to the gods of the story told
so you may have a voice.

Now Father,
I understand and
I've learned my lesson.

When I feel like giving up,

Artistic Narcissism
is the cure
for suicide.

And when I feel like giving up,

Artistic Suicide
is the cure for
narcissism.

"They may ignore you, but I'm burying these words,
in this Southern clay, so one day they will rise,
from the ground and outlive us all."
-LW